DESERTS

AN ACTIVITY GUIDE FOR AGES 6–9

Nancy F. Castaldo

CHICAGO
REVIEW
PRESS

Library of Congress Cataloging-in-Publication Data

Castaldo, Nancy F. (Nancy Fusco), 1962–

    Deserts : an activity guide for ages 6–9 / Nancy F. Castaldo.— 1st ed.
        p. cm.
    Includes bibliographical references (p.102) and index.
    ISBN 1-55652-524-9
    1. Deserts—Study and teaching (Elementary)—Activity programs
—Juvenile literature.   2. Desert ecology—Study and teaching
(Elementary)—Activity programs—Juvenile literature. [1. Deserts.
2. Desert ecology. 3. Ecology.]   I. Title.
    GB612.C38 2004
    372.35'7—dc22

                                        2003024104

Cover and interior design: Monica Baziuk
Cover and interior illustration: B. Kulak

Published by Chicago Review Press, Incorporated

814 North Franklin Street

Chicago, Illinois 60610

ISBN 1-55652-524-9

Printed in the United States of America

5   4   3   2   1

For my dad, Andrew, and his sisters, Ann, Barbara, and Terry,

who have always inspired me with their love of the desert

CONTENTS

ACKNOWLEDGMENTS

Many thanks to my parents for introducing me to the deserts of America. Thanks to Richard Hill of the Saguaro National Park for his knowledge of cacti and their protection, and Daniel Holland for his insight on Mongolia. Thanks to formerdesert-ratnowmidwesterngalpalandeditorextraordinaire Lisa Rosenthal for always making it fun; Betsy Kulak for making it beautiful; Monica Baziuk, Allison Felus, and Gerilee Hundt for putting it all together; and Cynthia Sherry for endless encouragement. And always to Dean and Lucie for their support, love, and readiness to explore new worlds.

INTRODUCTION

"Like a great poet, Nature knows how to produce the greatest effects with the most limited means."

—Heinrich Heine, 1797–1856

The poet Heinrich Heine wrote these words over 200 years ago. And if you have ever seen a sunset in a desert, you know that these words certainly ring true. The desert, sparse as it may seem, is breathtaking.

There are deserts all over our world. In fact, deserts cover about one-fifth of the earth's surface and many are still growing. Some are found near the equator and are hot and dry, while deserts to the far north are quite cold. They are usually thought to be barren lands with little plant or animal life, but over thousands of years many animals and plants have adapted. In the Sahara Desert alone there are an estimated 1,200 species of plants.

Deserts is written for everyone who is intrigued by these vast regions, whether or not you have visited one. Alone or in groups, kids will enjoy the activities that explore these mysterious lands. Readers will see the deserts unfold on these pages and discover the wonders that need preserving. Facts will pop out in Desert Discovery sidebars, and ideas for more fun appear in Desert Challenges at the end of the book. You'll also find additional ways to explore the deserts with recommended books, videos, and Web sites. A listing of places to visit and a calendar of yearly events will continue the desert fun. Most of all, kids will discover a new frontier that they'll want to continue to explore. So turn the page and start getting wild about deserts!

DISCOVERING 1 DESERTS

Close your eyes and imagine yourself in a desert. In the desert of your imagination you might find yourself under the sun and standing on hot sand. You might look up to see sand and rocks in all directions. At night the sand becomes colder and the cloudless sky becomes full of stars. Well, that is what you will find in many deserts, but not in all of them. About one-fifth of the surface of the earth is desert. Most deserts are just as you imagine—hot—but others are very cold. However, all deserts have one thing in common—very little rain.

The Biologist's View of the Desert

There are many ways to define a desert. Meteorologists define the desert by the amount of rainfall (or *precipitation*) it receives each year. By definition, a desert is a place that receives very little rain. In fact, the rain must be less than 19.7 inches (50 cm) each year. Look at a yardstick and see if you can find the 50-centimeter mark on the metric side. You'll see that it's an extremely small amount of rain for one whole year. Compare that to the total amount of precipitation for the Albany, New York, area in 2002 at 40.8 inches (103.6 cm), and you'll see that the desert receives a much smaller amount in one year. (What is the annual precipitation in your town?) Biologists look at rainfall when they define a desert, but in addition they look at the evaporation rate. *Evaporation* is when a liquid changes into a gas; in this case, the liquid is the rain. The evaporation rate describes the time it takes for the rain to dissipate into the air. The evaporation rate must be greater than the amount of rainfall for the region to be called a desert by biologists. Basically, biologists focus on the little amount of rain deserts receive each year and the fact that most of that rain evaporates and is not beneficial to the animals and plants that live in the region.

What Makes Most Deserts So Hot?

Why are most deserts so hot? Most deserts fall between the latitudes called the Tropic of Cancer and the Tropic of Capricorn. If you look on a globe, these *latitude* lines are found on either side of the equator. This region is known as a *subtropical climate belt*. Generally it has dry air and clear skies. The winds are very dry because they have lost most of their moisture in the more northern or southern regions. These deserts are often described as hot, dry deserts. The winds along their western coasts are often cooled by cold ocean currents, which cause them to drop only a small amount of water. These areas are called *coastal* deserts. Atacama, in Chile, is an example of a coastal desert.

Some deserts are found far inland or between mountains. Often these are known as *semiarid* deserts. Semiarid deserts are found in Utah, Montana, Russia, and northern Asia. The winds that reach these deserts have usually released most of their moisture before reaching the desert areas.

Desert regions also absorb more heat than humid regions. Since there is not much to deflect the sun's rays (bounce the rays off of the ground) in the desert, the desert absorbs 90 percent of the sun's rays, or solar radiation, which heats the ground and the layer of air above the ground. In more humid regions of the world the sun's rays are deflected by clouds, dust, and water.

Ghost Rains

In order for rain to fall there must be clouds in the sky. Clouds rarely float over the desert, but once in a while a cloud does float over the desert and rain falls to the hot ground below. Sometimes the ground is so hot that there is a layer of hot air just above the ground. This air can be so hot that it evaporates the rain as soon as the rain hits it. The rain never reaches the dry earth of the desert. When this occurs it is called a *ghost rain*. Sometimes a ghost rain cools the layer of hot air enough so that if a second rainfall occurs, this rain will not evaporate and will have a better chance of falling to the ground.

Make a Solar Still

Plants and animals that live in the desert have adapted to the lack of rain in very unique ways that we will explore further. People, however, do not have these adaptations. They have to obtain water or they will die. A person can live only about three days without water when the temperature is above 100°F (37.8°C), as it is in the hot and dry deserts.

There are only a handful of ways to obtain water in the desert. You could try to collect rainwater or dew in the morning. You could also get water from desert plants, like cacti. Another way to obtain water is to build a solar still. The solar still was created by two doctors and was tested by the United States Air Force in the deserts of Arizona. Here's how to make your own.

What You Need
- A grown-up to assist
- Shovel
- Measuring tape
- Glass jar, such as a 32-ounce (.9 liter) mayonnaise jar
- Plastic wrap
- Stones

What You Do
1. Dig a hole roughly 3 feet (.9 m) across and about 2 feet (.6 m) deep.
2. Place the open jar in the center of the hole with the opening on top.
3. Ask someone to help you spread a large sheet of plastic wrap over the hole and jar.

4. Place stones on the plastic wrap on the ground to hold it down, and place one stone in the center of the plastic wrap covering the jar opening to hold the plastic wrap securely over the opening of the jar. Water will eventually gather in the jar through the process of condensation. *Condensation* occurs when the water vapor in the air is pulled out and turned into liquid water. You might get a pint of water in about 24 hours.

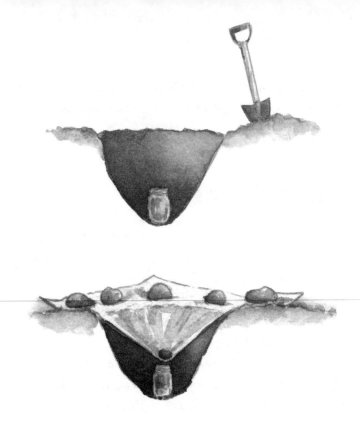

If you were trying to survive in the desert, your body would require about seven to eight pints (3.3 to 3.8 L) of water each day you are exerting energy. You could probably last about five days without water if you didn't exert any energy at all. That means no walking, not even at night. Look at the water you gathered in your still. Would it be enough for you to survive until you are rescued? Would it be enough to sustain you walking at night to search for help?

Desert Discovery

The still not only collects water, it purifies it. Here's something important to remember if you are making your still in the desert and you have no other water: One still can keep you alive; making more stills will keep your friends alive as well.

People of the Desert

It is difficult to imagine people living in the extreme conditions of the desert. While people are not built for life in the desert, they have found ways to adapt to life in deserts around the world for thousands of years. How do these people protect themselves from the harsh climate? Just as hair or fur can benefit desert animals, clothing sometimes protects people from the extreme temperatures of the desert.

What do you do when you are very hot? You might put on a bathing suit or shorts and a T-shirt to cool yourself down. Some desert people wear very little clothing, but some others put on loose-fitting, flowing garments that shield their bodies from the heat and cold and also help to reduce evaporation through the skin. In the following chapters you will see how the different people of the deserts have adjusted to the harsh desert conditions.

Wind and Water at Work

Deserts have dramatic landscapes with many unique land formations. There are rugged cliffs, giant sand dunes, rock columns and arches, and colorful canyons. With little soil or vegetation to offer protection, these spectacular formations are often caused by winds ripping across the desert, carrying sand and gravel that cuts and carves out desert landforms. Some of these

landforms, such as the Rainbow Bridge National Monument in Arizona, are so dramatic that they have become world-famous attractions for visitors from all over the world. The Rainbow Bridge, made of sandstone, is the world's largest natural bridge and spans Bridge Canyon. Can you name any canyons or other landmarks that attract a lot of visitors?

Let's take a look at some other landforms. You might have heard of *mesas* and *buttes*. These two types of formations are sometimes used as landmarks by desert travelers. In the vast desert landscape they help travelers identify their locations. They also help to produce some of the desert's spectacular scenery. Both mesas and buttes jut out of the flat desert toward the sky. Mesas are large plateaus that have steep sides and look a little like flattened mountains. When mesas erode they become buttes. Buttes are smaller, isolated forms that also have steep cliffs or slopes.

Other landforms include *playas* and *salt flats*. Playas are temporary lakes that form in the desert. When these lakes dry up they form salt flats. We'll take another look at salt flats on our journey to South America.

Desert Plants

To survive the harsh conditions plants face every day in the desert, they must adapt in various ways. They may not have to compete for light and space, as they do in the forest, but instead they must compete for water. Some plants store water, while others can locate underground water. Still others have adapted to living with very little water.

Most plants in the desert seem to hug the ground. Unlike the rainforest, where there is a large canopy of leaves and layers of plants, the hot, dry desert has mostly low-growing shrubs and short, woody trees and plants, such as cacti and mesquite. Being close to the ground helps these plants retain moisture so that the wind does not dry them out, which would happen if these plants were taller.

Sagebrush, a low-growing plant and Nevada's state flower, is common in the semiarid deserts of Utah and Montana and, of course, Nevada, where it carpets the ground for miles. Sagebrush is also found in cold deserts.

Coastal deserts have plants that have adapted with stems that swell when water is available and shrink when it's not. Most of these plants have roots close to the surface that can soak up rainwater before it drains into the ground. Plants that grow in these deserts include rice grass, little leaf horsebrush, black sage, and saltbush. All of these plants have individual adaptations. The saltbush, for example, has the ability to continue making sugars in extreme heat, when most plants shut down their food processes.

Spiny Shadows

You can't say that desert plants don't have attitude, because they really do. There are other plants that protect themselves from animals that can eat them, but not many go so far as to grow spines that say, "No munching here," such as cacti. Cacti are part of the group of desert plants known as *succulents*, and they range in size from 50-foot (15.2-m) saguaros to cacti that are the size of a thumbnail, such as the *Blossfeldia liliputana*, which only grows about a half inch (1.3 cm) across. All cacti are succulents, but not all succulents are cacti. Succulents have thick, fleshy stems or leaves that store water. Cacti grow in hot, dry deserts and semiarid deserts. Typically cacti have round or cylindrical shapes and spiny surfaces. These spines protect the plant from munching animals. Spines can also help keep the cactus cool. In this activity you will make your own cactus model to see how this happens.

What You Need
 Clay
 Flashlight
Toothpicks

What You Do

1. First, mold your clay into the shape of a cactus. You can easily form the shape of a barrel cactus by making a ball of clay, then flattening the bottom so that it can stand up on its own on a flat surface.

2. Shine the flashlight on the cactus you formed. As you will see, all of the light reaches the surface of the cactus, just as the sun would in the desert.

3. Now start adding toothpicks to the cactus to form the spines. Poke the toothpicks all around the surface of the cactus.

4. Shine the flashlight on the spiny cactus. Does all the light reach the surface of the cactus? Can you see how the spines of the cactus can shade a cactus and keep it from overheating and getting burned by the sun?

Blossfeldia liliputana

Create a Cactus

You can actually create your own cactus with a method that gardeners use called *grafting*. Grafting is a process that adds one plant to another plant to develop a new plant that is unique. Sometimes this is done to save a plant that is in danger of dying, and other times this is done to create a unique variation. Sometimes certain kinds of cacti are difficult to grow and it's easier to obtain the plant through this process. This project should be done in the summer when the cacti are in their growing season.

What You Need

- A grown-up to assist
- 2 different cactus plants
- A clean, sharp knife
- Toothpicks

What You Do

1. Pick out the cactus that will be the base for your new plant. You will need a grown-up to cut the top off of that cactus. The base should remain rooted in the soil.

2. Ask a grown-up to cut the top of the other cactus off, making sure that both cut areas are about the same size.

3. Place the top of the second cactus on the bottom that is still rooted in the soil. Line the two portions up so that they match pretty well.

Desert Discovery

Some cacti, such as the hedgehog cactus and barrel cactus, have a dense covering of silvery spines. The spines not only provide shade for the cacti, but their color also helps to deflect the sun's rays from the cactus plant. In addition, some cacti have very small jets between their spines that spray water from within the cactus to its surface. This acts like a sprinkler system to help cool the plant in the hot desert sun.

4. Insert a toothpick to hold the two together. Place the new cactus in a shady spot for a couple of days.

5. After a couple of days, place your new cactus in a sunny spot and follow your regular cactus care. Make sure not to pull the pieces apart to check them.

6. Allow about two weeks for the cacti pieces to become fully grafted.

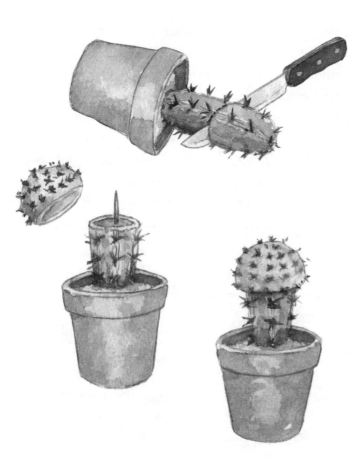

Desert Discovery

There is a custom of people bringing a candle, a loaf of bread, and some salt to the owners of a new house. The candle signifies that there should always be light, the bread symbolizes that there should always be food, and the salt symbolizes the spice of life everyone needs. The Hopi Indians of the American Sonoran Desert have their own custom. They put pieces of cactus in the corners of each new house to "give the house roots." Can you think of any customs like that in your family?

Sandy Soil Experiment

Plants that grow in the desert must not only adapt to the heat, they must also adapt to sandy soil. Try this experiment to see what happens to seeds in sandy desert soil.

What You Need

- 2 small terra-cotta pots
- Sand
- Garden soil
- Lettuce seeds
- Water

What You Do

1. Place sand in the first pot and ordinary soil from your garden in the second pot.

2. Plant the lettuce seeds in each pot and water.

3. Place the two pots on a sunny windowsill and water them every three to four days.

4. Keep a record of the plants' growth. What do you notice? Does one grow faster than the other? How often do the pots dry out?

Animals Also Make a Home in the Desert

There aren't many large animals that live in deserts because most animals are not able to store enough

water and tolerate the heat. Instead, in the hot and dry deserts there are mostly small animals like kangaroo rats and other animals that can burrow or dig into the ground during the day and come out at night when it's cooler. Of course, there are always exceptions.

Each desert has its own variety of animals. Badgers and coyotes are able to live comfortably in the semiarid desert regions. They're joined by owls and eagles. Kangaroo rats, jackrabbits, gerbils, and a few species of mice also make their home in desert regions. Many reptile and insect species have also adapted to the extremes of desert weather.

The key to searching out most desert critters is that you have to do it at night. The desert may seem barren during the day, but it often comes alive at night. One resort in the American Southwest desert region actually supplies its guests with night-vision goggles to see the desert wilderness at its most active time of the day.

Start the Journey

It's time to begin our journey, and what better place to start than right here at home in the American deserts. For some of you, this might not require more than stepping outside your front door. Just remember to wear comfortable shoes, a hat with a large brim, and sunglasses, and bring a water bottle!

WELCOME TO 2 THE WILD WEST

We are beginning our desert journey right at home in the United States. There are four desert regions in the United States: the Sonoran Desert, Mojave Desert, Great Basin Desert, and Chihuahuan Desert. All of these are found in the western region. If you look on a map of the United States you will see that most are actually in the southwestern area of the country.

For many desert travelers, the desert is a source of anxiety and mystery. For some people, everything about the desert, from the extreme weather conditions to the snakes that they may find, runs contradictory to their feelings of home and safety. But for others who understand the desert, it is a magical place, full of interesting things to explore and wildlife to encounter, and, yes, it's even a place to live. So let's begin this journey of desert discovery in the great Southwest.

The Sonoran

Let's begin with the hottest of American deserts—the Sonoran Desert. This arid desert covers 120,000 square miles (310,000 sq km) in southeastern California, the southwest region of Arizona, most of Baja California, and half of the state of Sonora, Mexico. Although this is the hottest desert in the United States, with daily temperatures frequently ranging from 90°F to over 100°F (32.2°C to 37.8°C), it has the most variety of life, or greatest *biodiversity*, of the American deserts. This is partially because unlike the other American deserts, the Sonoran has mild winters and rarely experiences any frosts. This desert is unique because of its brief rainy seasons that occur periodically between December and March, and between July and mid-September. There are poppies, lupines, and other wildflowers, and cacti, mesquite, and other shrubs. In fact, there are roughly 2,000 plant species represented in this desert region. There are even trees, such as Arizona Ash, cottonwood, and willows.

Saguaro Time Line

One of the most visible inhabitants of the American deserts, and unique to the Sonoran desert, is the *saguaro* (sah-WAH-ro) cactus. Like other cactus plants, the saguaro is a succulent and has spines. The saguaro is able to store water in its stem. Like some other types of cactus plants, it has a pleated trunk. During times of drought, when water is very scarce, the trunk becomes thin, but after it rains the trunk expands to store more water to use in times of drought or the dry season. The saguaro grows very slowly. In fact, it takes a saguaro cactus about ten years just to grow from seed to one and a half inches (4 cm) tall. It may be a slow grower, but it can live 175 to 200 years.

A saguaro starts with a single seed and can eventually grow to weigh 6 to 7 tons (5.4 to 6.3 t), which is about the weight of a car, and be 50 feet (15.24 m) tall. Its roots may extend into the soil only four inches (10.16 cm). Can you believe that such a big cactus has such shallow roots? But these roots are able to really soak up the rainwater as soon as it hits the ground; if the roots were deeper, then the rain wouldn't reach them.

It's easy to draw a saguaro cactus and make your own time line to see how this giant of the desert grows over the years. Here's how.

What You Need

 Paper

 Colored pencils

What You Do

1. Use the picture to the right as a guide to draw your own saguaro cactus.

2. Draw a line at the top of your cactus and label it 200 years. At the bottom of your cactus draw another line and label it *seed* or 0 years.

3. Now fill in the middle years of your cactus with other lines. At 10 years the cactus would only be about 4 inches (10.2 cm) tall, so draw the line just a little bit above the ground. At 25 years the cactus would be about 2 feet (.6 m) high. At 50 years old the cactus would reach 10 feet (3 m) high. At 60 years it would reach 18 feet (5.5 m) high. At 150 years it would reach 50 feet (15.2 m).

4. After you make your time line, use the colored pencils to show what your cactus looks like as it grows up. The saguaro is green, and at 50 years white flowers with yellow centers start to bloom on the cactus. The flowers grow at the top of the plant and bloom at night. Why do you think the flowers bloom at night instead of during the day? When a saguaro is about 60 years old, animals, such as owls, begin to make the cactus their home. They nest in holes inside the cactus created by woodpeckers, insects, and other animals. By the time the cactus is 150 years old there are many holes all over it.

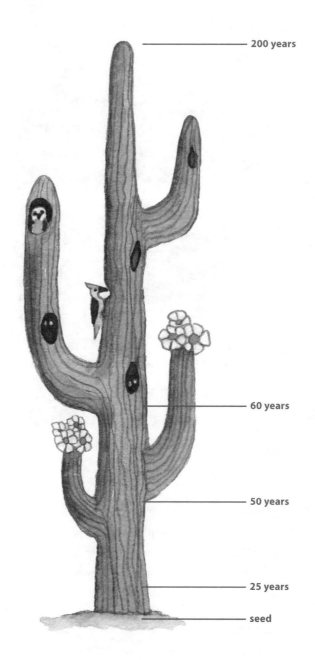

200 years

60 years

50 years

25 years

seed

Saguaro Protection

Efforts to protect saguaro cacti and other native plants from collection and damage have led to laws in Arizona that require individuals to obtain a permit from the state to remove or relocate any native plant on their property. That even holds true for a property owner who wants to move a cactus from one end of their property to the other. The property owner must present their land deed, obtain a permit, and then tag the plant during relocation. And if a developer plans on clearing land to build, the state may require a nursery to come in and salvage the native plants on that land before any building can begin.

Saguaro cactus

Desert Discovery

A saguaro can produce 40 million seeds during its lifetime, but chances are that only one of those seeds will grow into an adult cactus. Tiny seeds that are able to survive are often sheltered from the hot sun, winter cold, and predators by other desert plants.

A Saguaro Called the Grand One

When Lewis and Clark set off to explore the West in 1804, the Grand One was just a little saguaro seedling in Arizona. Today the Grand One has seen its 200th birthday and its share of hot summers and strong winds. It's now over 46 feet (14 m) high, which is the reason the saguaro was noticed in 2002 by cactus spotters Joe Pleggenkuhle and his grandson, Chris Seymour. They and another cactus spotter, Chuck Hockaday, reported the sightings to the American Forests National Register of Big Trees. (Cactus spotters and tree spotters are people who are on the lookout for big trees and cacti. Anyone can be a spotter. Look at the Web site in the Desert Resources section for more details.)

If the Grand One, as it is called, turns out to be the biggest saguaro in America it will be officially crowned in 2004. So keep your eyes peeled—you might spot an even bigger one!

Coral Snake Bracelet

The brightly colored coral snake is one of the more dangerous inhabitants of the Sonoran Desert. It lives in rocky areas where saguaro cacti are prevalent. The coral snake is a relative of the cobra and has a bite more lethal than a rattlesnake.

Coral snakes are small, only about 13 to 22 inches (33 to 55.9 cm) in length. They are *nocturnal*, like many desert creatures, meaning they are active at night. Their bands of color are easy to recognize and act as a warning. Perhaps the snake's size, markings, and nocturnal habits have contributed to the fact that there are no known human deaths associated with this snake.

The scarlet king snake has similar markings, but the coral snake is the only snake that has red bands bordered by either pale yellow or white. Create this bracelet to help remind you of the colors of the coral snake. Make an extra one for a friend.

What You Need
- 6-inch (15.2-cm) piece of elastic
- Beads—yellow, red, and black

What You Do

1. String the beads onto the elastic in the order of their colors on the coral snake—yellow, red, yellow, black, yellow, red, yellow. Repeat the pattern almost the full length of your elastic or enough to wrap around your wrist.

2. Tie the ends of your bracelet together and slip it onto your wrist. Wear it as a reminder to alert someone if you see a snake that matches those colors on a desert visit.

How the Rattlesnakes Came to Be

This Zuni tale explains the origin of rattlesnakes.

Many, many years ago there lived many rattlesnakes, but then the rattlesnakes were men and women, not like the snakes we know today. One day a group of rattlesnake children went out to play by the banks of a river. They asked if they could take their youngest sister to play with them. "You may take your sister with you," said their mother. "But you must be very careful with her because she is very small." The children all agreed to be careful with their little sister.

When they reached the river they began taking turns sliding down the banks, one after another. The little sister ran after the older children, clapping her hands and laughing, down the steep bank. *The oldest child called out to her to stop, but the little sister was too young to understand the warnings. Just then the little sister fell and began rolling down the hill, and as she did, she got smaller and smaller, thinner and thinner.*

The children all gathered around their little sister and cried, "Rattlesnake, rattlesnake, little, little!" They carried their sister home and everyone who saw the little sister also cried, "Rattlesnake, rattlesnake, little, little!"

The little girl's mother fell to the ground in despair. The children then fell to the ground in despair. They stayed that way for such a long time so that to this day, rattlesnakes still wriggle along the ground, crying in despair.

So you see that once these rattlesnakes were people— splendid people. That is why we do not kill them needlessly.

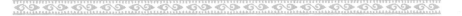

Desert Discovery

Hopi Indians perform a spiritual dance called the snake dance. It is danced as a prayer for rain. Snake priests hold live snakes as they dance. The Hopi believe that the snakes are messengers of the underworld and can help assure them of rainfall for their crops and spring water to drink.

Slithering in the Sand

There are other snakes that live in the deserts of the United States besides the coral and the king snakes. Some, like the rattlesnake, are poisonous and should be avoided at all costs. A number of rattlesnakes live in the deserts, including the diamondback and the sidewinder. The rattlers are dangerous, and their bite can cause a fatality, but rattlers are all easily recognizable by the rattle at the end of their tail and the noise they make. Other snakes, like the nonpoisonous gopher snakes and whipsnakes, are not as dangerous. It's best to avoid any snake you see in the wild.

Here are some tips to avoid an attack if you do come across a dangerous snake:

1. Never poke at a snake to get it to move.

2. While facing the snake, back away from it slowly. Make sure it has a way out.

3. Never corner a snake.

4. Wear long pants, socks, and sturdy shoes if you are hiking in an area that has poisonous snakes.

5. Never pick up a rock or a log with your hands. Kick it over first with your boot or a stick in case a snake is resting underneath. Of course, snakes aren't the only desert creatures to be wary of. Scorpions are also on the loose and should be avoided.

Desert Discovery

The ancestors of our modern snakes appeared in the Triassic period along with the first dinosaurs about 200 million years ago. The snakes we are more familiar with today are said to have evolved from lizards in the Cretaceous period about 130 million years ago. This is mostly theory due to the lack of fossil evidence. Unfortunately, fossils of these early snakes are rare because their small, delicate bones tended to break down or scatter.

Coral snake

On a visit to a United States desert you might see lizards, kangaroo rats, owls, and many other creatures, but not camels. Camels live in other deserts of the world today, but long ago camels actually roamed this land as well. The 100,000-year-old fossilized remains of a North American camel were discovered in Long Beach, California, in 2002. Camels originated on this continent 15 million years ago. As they died out here, they spread to the continent of Africa and to the Middle East, which is where they still live today.

Finding Fossils

The desert is filled with evidence of prehistoric life. *Paleontologists*, scientists who study dinosaurs, have uncovered many bones from these prehistoric creatures. Bones of three-toed horses, saber-toothed tigers, and even elephants can be found embedded in rock formations. Others can be found in sediment.

Visit the Petrified Forest National Park in Arizona and you will find evidence that this region was a lush forest in the Triassic Period (200 to 250 million years ago). Some of those trees have been fossilized into beautiful, colorful logs that can be seen today.

Although petrified wood can be found in many other places, this forest is considered to be the best preserved and most beautiful collection in the world.

Fossils are fun to look for in the desert. Here are some tips on finding some on your next visit:

1. Look at the foot-high mounds of harvester ants in the desert regions of Colorado to find the fossil teeth of sharks and other sea creatures. Ancient seas covered the deserts of America millions of years ago.

2. Look at rocky outcroppings, where highways are cut through rock. If you can see the different layers of the rock there might be limestone, sandstone, or shale. These rocks, known as sedimentary rock, are where most fossils are found.

3. Bring along a fossil field guide that will help you identify what you find. (See the Desert Resources section.)

4. When you do find a fossil, look at it, but don't take it with you. Every fossil that is taken out of a park removes important historical and environmental information. Plenty of fossils, taken from private lands, are available for purchase at the park gift shops.

5. Record your find by taking a picture of it or by making a rubbing, using a pencil and paper.

The Mojave

The Mojave Desert lies between the hot Sonoran Desert and the cooler Great Basin Desert. This arid desert covers 25,000 square miles (64,100 sq km) of southeastern California, Arizona, Utah, and Nevada. Las Vegas and the famous Death Valley, one of the hottest places on earth and a national park, are both found in the Mojave Desert. It is well known for its dramatic scenery and the fact that it is the lowest, hottest, and driest spot in North America. The temperature can reach 131°F (55°C) during the day. The ground can be even hotter: 174°F (79°C), which is so hot it can actually burn your feet.

The Mojave is home to yucca, creosote bushes, desert tortoises, and Joshua trees. There are very few succulents in this desert. Larger animals, such as coyotes and bighorn sheep, also call the Mojave home, as do many birds, insects, and reptiles. There is a winter rainy season, and hard frosts are common here.

People of the Desert

Many Native Americans made their home in the desert. The Hopi and the other Pueblo Native Americans lived for thousands of years in the hot desert area of what originally was called the Great Basin. They lived in villages and farmed rather than hunted for their food. Farming was difficult in some of these areas, so they developed ways of using floodwaters to irrigate their crops, such as corn. Perhaps one of the most well-known aspects of these ancient people was their architecture. The Pueblo tribes built their homes of stone or adobe mud with thick walls and small windows that helped shade and insulate their homes from the harsh desert climate. (Many modern home designs in Arizona and New Mexico are inspired by this Pueblo design.)

Desert Discovery

In 1862 Kit Carson and his soldiers, under the direction of General James Carleton, began burning Navajo crops and homes in an effort to rid the territory of Native Americans. Mexicans, along with Ute and Pueblo volunteers, took their revenge on the Navajo for earlier raids by joining the soldiers. This culminated in the 300-mile (482.8-km) trek, known as the Long Walk, to move the Navajo to a camp at Fort Sumner in New Mexico. There were many more struggles between the Native Americans and the United States government. Some have been settled, while others are still in dispute. Today the Navajo nation has grown from the 8,000 left after the Long Walk to more than 210,000. Find out more about the Navajo who still live in the Southwest in the Desert Resources section.

Over the centuries different groups, including the Apaches, Spaniards, Mexicans, and Americans, drove the Pueblo natives from their territories. Today their descendants can still be found in the region and their pueblos still stand in many places of the desert. Look in the Desert Resources section for places to see these pueblos.

Navajo Sand Painting

Tribal leaders create Navajo sand paintings for the purpose of healing. They use crushed stone, flowers, pollen, and other natural items from the desert to create their design on the ground. Some sand paintings are also created as art to hang on walls. Here's how you can create your own sand painting.

What You Need

- A grown-up to assist
- Sandpaper
- Pencil
- Sand
- Empty jars
- Powdered tempera paints
- Craft sticks
- White craft glue
- Spray fixative

What You Do

1. Draw a simple picture on the rough side of the sandpaper with your pencil.

2. Place some sand in each of the jars. Add just a tiny bit of tempera paint to each jar (one color per jar). Mix with a craft stick. Add more paint if you need the color to be darker.

3. Use another craft stick to spread glue onto each section of your picture where you want the first color of sand to be. Sprinkle the first color of sand onto the picture. Be sure the sand covers all the glue. Lift the picture up and tilt it to remove the excess sand.

4. Continue painting your picture with the sand in each color until your picture is complete. Remove the excess sand in between each new color.

5. Let your sand painting dry completely and then ask a grown-up to spray it with a fixative.

Hopi Kachina

Hopi children learn about kachinas as part of their spiritual educations. The word *kachina* means three different but related things to Native Americans of the Southwest. First, it is a term to describe spirits that visit the tribes. Second, it describes masked dancers who represent the kachinas when they visit the human world. Last, the word refers to the small wooden dolls that are painted to represent the kachina spirit beings.

During ceremonies the masked kachina dancers give kachina dolls to children in the tribe to teach them about the different kachina spirits. The children hang the dolls on the walls of their home to remind them of the many different spirits. The Hopi recognize over 250 different kachina spirits, including the Owl Kachina, Sun Kachina, Butterfly Maiden, and Corn Kachina. Each spirit has its own story and lesson to teach the Hopi children.

Here's how to create your own kachina doll with materials that are easy to find.

What You Need
 Toilet paper roll, or paper-towel roll cut in half
Pencil
Acrylic paint
Paintbrush
Paper
Scissors
Glue
Optional: Feathers, fabric, beads, and other decorations

What You Do

1. Decide what type of kachina doll you want to make. Do you want to create a cactus kachina, a sun kachina, or another kind of kachina? When you have decided, outline

Kachina dolls

the kachina's body shape on the cardboard tube with a pencil.

2. Fill in the body shape with the paints. Let dry.

3. Outline the body with black paint. Let dry.

4. Draw the kachina's head on a sheet of paper, then cut it out.

5. Paint the head and let it dry.

6. Glue the head onto the top of the cardboard tube body.

7. Add any other decorations you want to finish your kachina doll.

The Great Basin Desert

This is the most northern of the four American deserts. This region covers 190,000 square miles (487,200 km). It lies between the Rocky Mountains, the Sierra Nevada, and the Cascade Mountains. This desert includes parts of California, Idaho, Utah, and Oregon, as well as large parts of Nevada. It's the region where the Grand Canyon is found.

High elevations of at least 3,000 feet (914 m) and its northern location make this desert the coldest in the United States. Winter precipitation often falls as snow instead of rain. Unlike some of the other deserts, this desert doesn't have a rainy season, but rather the rainfall is distributed throughout the year and only measures between 7 and 12 inches (17.8 cm and 30.5 cm) annually. It has very few trees and succulents. Instead you'll find a lot of sagebrush growing.

Desert Discovery
This desert is called the Great Basin because all of the waterways that are found in this region flow into the desert flats and not into the sea.

The Grand Canyon

Located in northern Arizona, the Grand Canyon National Park is one of the most visited sites in the United States. It encompasses 277 miles (445.7 km) of the Colorado River and adjacent lands, and over one million acres. The canyon itself is a deep chasm, in some places reaching 6,000 feet (1,828 m) deep, carved out of the Colorado Plateau by the Colorado River over a million years ago. It is one of the greatest examples of desert erosion in the world. Inside the canyon are caves that contain archeological, biological, and geological resources that provide scientists with a rich history of the region.

The entire park is considered semiarid desert, although there are different habitats at different park elevations, such as pine forests and sandy beaches. There are over 300 species of birds, 47 reptile species, 89 animal species, and even a number of fish and amphibians that make their home in the canyon. Over the years people have also played a part in shaping this ecosystem. Nonnative species have been introduced to the park and have competed with native canyon wildlife. Air pollution has drifted over and blocked canyon visibility, and construction of nearby dams and other projects have also impacted the park. This has led to the introduction of many laws to protect this American treasure. For example, scrubbers installed in the smokestacks of coal-fired power plants have reduced air pollution. Park management is now using a variety of tools to relocate or kill nonnative and pest species that are harming native plants and animals. Some areas of the park are even off-limits to planes flying overhead in an effort to protect the peaceful tranquility of the canyon for visitors.

The Chihuahuan Desert

This southernmost desert in the United States, located in Arizona and New Mexico, is at a high elevation—on average, between 3,000 (914 m) and 5,000 feet (1,524 m). At this high elevation, arctic winds contribute to the hard frosts that are common here. It is roughly 200,000 square miles in area, with most desert lands lying south of the United States border in Mexico. The average annual rainfall is 17 inches (43.2 cm). Cool winter temperatures and very hot summers are characteristic of this region. The temperature in the winter falls below freezing on average 100 times during the year, but in summer the temperature can reach 122°F (50°C).

Plant life here is similar to the plant life in the Great Basin, with many shrubs and grasses. In addition, yucca plants and agaves can also be found. Prickly pears are prevalent.

Prickly Pears: Fruit and Fried

Although the prickly pear cactus is abundant in the Chihuahuan desert, it is found in all the deserts of the United States, as well as in Mexico and parts of the Mediterranean. The cactus produces fruits that you can find in the produce section of your supermarket. These prickly pears come in different varieties: yellow, purple, and white. Not only are the fruits edible and sweet, the pads of the cactus are also edible. Check out some of the sites in the Desert Resources section for recipes.

Before eating a prickly pear you must first peel it. You won't have to worry about spines if you purchase it at the local supermarket, because these are removed before the prickly pears are put out for sale, but if you purchase prickly pears or pads from a farm stand, follow the directions for peeling the spines, listed here.

What You Need

- A grown-up to assist
- Prickly pear
- Bowl
- Water
- Tongs
- Paper towels
- Paring knife

What You Do

1. Place the fruit in a bowl of water to remove some of the spines.
2. Lift the prickly pear with the tongs and place it on two paper towels.
3. Have a grown-up hold the prickly pear with the paper towels and slice through its skin with the paring knife, as if peeling a potato.
4. Use the paper towels to help peel away the skin from the fruit. Have the grown-up cut the peeled fruit into long slices or finger-length strands to eat or to use in a recipe.

Fried prickly pear cactus is a traditional Native American treat enjoyed by many tribes. You can make this version using cactus pads that have been prepared and canned for use in recipes. They are called *nopalitos* in Spanish. Here's how.

What You Need

- A grown-up to assist
- 1 can or jar of nopalitos (found in Latin American or Mexican markets)
- Sea salt
- Paper bag
- 1 cup (125 g or 200 ml) cornmeal
- 5 tablespoons (75 ml) peanut oil
- Frying pan
- Tongs

- Paper towels
- Plate

What You Do

1. Rinse the nopalitos. If they are not in strips, ask a grown-up to cut them up for you.
2. Sprinkle a little bit of salt on them and place them in the paper bag.
3. Add the cornmeal to the bag and shake.
4. Ask a grown-up to heat the oil in the frying pan, then add the nopalitos.
5. Use the tongs to turn the nopalitos when the bottoms turn brown.
6. Place the paper towels on the plate. Place the browned nopalitos on the paper towels to drain them.
7. Serve with salsa and enjoy!

Exploring the Past

Paleontologists are not the only scientists working in the American deserts to discover evidence of its past. Archeologists are also hard at work exploring the remains of Native Americans, ancestors of the Navajo, Hopi, and Apache people who live there today, who made the desert their home almost a thousand years ago. Visitors to American deserts don't have to be

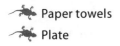

Desert Discovery
Navajo, also spelled Navaho, is the name of both a large Native American nation and the people of that nation. The Hopi live on an Indian reservation within the Navajo nation. Navajo people call themselves *Diné*, which means "people" in the Navajo language.

archeologists, though, to see the pueblos or homes that many tribes built and that still remain in the Southwest. These early people also left behind *petroglyphs*, or pictures on the desert rocks.

Petroglyph Pendant

Petroglyphs are designs and pictures created by desert natives, who carved or scratched the dark layer of rock away to reveal the lighter rock. Think about the pictures you draw. You probably draw pictures of your friends, or maybe animals and other things that interest you. The ancient people of the pueblos drew what interested them in the desert. They drew pictures to mark an important event, like a successful hunt, to tell a story, and sometimes to mark a trail to a food source or water. Take a trip to the Petroglyph National Monument in Albuquerque, New Mexico, and you will probably see plenty of these drawings—there are more than 25,000 images recorded at the site. More than 20 tribes have been connected with this sacred place in New Mexico over the centuries, each one contributing their own petroglyphs. If you can't get there in person, check out the Web site listed in the Desert Resources section.

You can make your own petroglyph design using clay. Here's how.

What You Need
 Sculpy or other polymer clay, any 2 colors (available in craft stores)

 Toothpick

What You Do

1. Choose two different colors of clay. Form the lighter shade into a ball the size of a large gumball.

2. Flatten the ball on a hard surface.

3. Roll the darker clay into a ball, then flatten it on a hard surface.

4. Place the lighter flattened clay in the middle of the flattened darker clay.

5. Gently pull up the darker clay and wrap it over the lighter clay so that the lighter clay is completely covered.

6. Use your toothpick to trim the clay into a pendant shape.

7. Begin drawing your design on the clay with your toothpick. Press down far enough into the clay so that you reveal the lighter clay.

8. Finish your pendant by making a hole in the top and baking the clay according to the directions on the clay package.

Travel On

Deserts do not recognize borders. They flow from country to country, as we can see with the Chihuahuan Desert, which extends into Mexico. There are three more deserts in South America. Let's travel south in the next chapter to explore the next group of American deserts.

SOUTH OF 3 THE BORDER

The deserts in South America are not as easy to explore as the deserts we explored in the United States because they are more difficult to reach. But they are certainly worth visiting. There is the Patagonian Desert of Argentina, which is similar in many ways to the Sonoran Desert, and the Atacama Desert of Northern Chile, which is often compared to the rolling, yellow-brown, rocky surface of Mars.

These deserts are amazing, but they also have their share of problems. One problem facing them is desertification.

Desertification

Desertification happens when deserts spread and become unable to support life. This happens through misuse of land at the edge of the desert. This misuse can be caused by poor farming practices, as we'll explore further in chapter 9. Misuse causes the land to change into a more barren and dry area that can no longer support plants and animals, as can natural deserts. Instead, such areas become wastelands. The land on the outskirts of the deserts of South America and other deserts is in danger of desertification. Let's begin our South American journey at the very bottom of South America, in a land sometimes called "the ends of the earth"—Patagonia.

Desert Discovery

The people of Patagonia are an interesting mix. Many people moved to Patagonia during the 1960s as hippies. Many affluent or rich people have also come to Patagonia over the last few decades to buy up land and build large homes. There are also many people who are descended from Welsh people who colonized Patagonia over a hundred years ago. People from all walks of life are still moving to Patagonia. The one thing they all have in common is a pioneering spirit. They come to Patagonia to be closer to nature, to lead healthy lives, and to fulfill their personal dreams, just like people did hundreds of years ago.

The Ends of the Earth

Patagonia is a huge region, and not all of it is desert. Patagonia covers about a third of the country of Argentina, which is the eighth largest country in the world. There are five provinces (equivalent to our states) covering 300,000 square miles (777,000 sq km). The Patagonian Desert is in the central region of Patagonia. To get there from the west we have to cross over mountains and rivers. We can also arrive through the Patagonian coasts, which are the most accessible and most frequently visited area of Patagonia, and which contain a tremendous amount of marine life.

The desert is less visited, but it has its own unique beauty and treasures. It is very much like the majority of deserts we visit. There is little rain and dry air. This occurs in Patagonia because rain clouds that form over the Pacific Ocean are stopped by the height of the mountains and are not able to move forward over the land. The desert is not sandy, but shrubby, with dried grass and thickets of thorns.

In Patagonia, man has contributed to this desert's growth by letting goats and sheep eat away most of the vegetation and by cutting down bushes for firewood.

Llama Mama Weaving

We saw that many, many years ago there were camels living in North America. There are still members of the camel family living in South America. The "camels of the clouds," as they are often called in this mountainous region, are the vicuña, llama, alpaca, and guanaco. Vicuña are the smallest camels, weighing only about 90 pounds and standing about three feet (.9 m) tall.

Alpacas and llamas are the two members of the South American camel family that were *domesticated*; in other words, they were trained and bred to work for man. The guanaco and vicuña are their wild cousins, and they still live in herds in the wild.

Their fleece keeps camels cool in the hot desert and warm when it is cold. It is also very soft and has been used for centuries by the people of Peru for clothing and blankets. Here's a simple belt that you can make using yarn made from alpaca or llama fleece.

What You Need
- A grown-up to assist
- Scissors
- 3 plastic drinking straws
- Measuring tape
- Yarn (visit a yarn store for alpaca or llama yarn, or use wool)

What You Do
1. Cut each straw in half.
2. Use the measuring tape to measure your waist for a belt. Add 10 more inches (25.4 cm) to that measurement.
3. Cut six lengths of yarn the length you calculated in step number 2.
4. Thread each length of yarn through one of the straws and knot the end so that the yarn can't fall back through the straw.
5. Tie all the strings together in one loose knot at the bottom. This is your loom. You are ready to begin weaving.
6. Begin weaving with a 2-foot-long (.6-m) length of yarn. Hold the straws in your hand (if you have trouble holding them you can tape them together until you've woven the

yarn a bit) and weave the length of yarn up and over each straw and then back again.

7. Keep on weaving until you finish that piece of yarn. Add another by knotting the new piece to the end of the one that you have just woven.

8. After you have covered the straws with the weaved yarn push the weaving down onto the loose strings. Keep on weaving until you reach the desired length of your belt.

9. To finish the belt, push all the weaving onto the strings, then cut the strings just below the knots. Remove the straws. Tie every two strings together in a double knot.

10. Trim the fringe to an even length and you're done! If you used alpaca or llama yarn, feel how soft your finished belt is. See if you can compare it to something made of wool.

Vicuña

Coquena and the Vicuña

In South American folklore, Coquena is the god who protects the vicuña. He is said to be a little man dressed in white who shepherds large herds of vicuña and punishes those who hurt them.

Patagonia's Other Residents

Camels are among the few animals able to survive in the Patagonian Desert. There are also some small animals that live mostly underground, like the tuco-tuco, which eats roots and grasses. This strangely named guinea pig–like rodent gets its name from the cries it makes when it senses danger. The cries echo all through the animal's tunnels to alert others. The tuco-tuco is about 15 inches (31.8 cm) long, including the tail, and weighs about a pound (.45 kg). Another rodent that calls Patagonia home is the agouti. The agouti lives alone mostly, instead of in a group like many other rodents. It has thick reddish-brown fur, which helps the animal look larger than it really is. Groups of mara rodents, which are very much like guinea pigs, also live here.

High above the desert fly the vulture hawks, which prey on the rodents and even smaller hawks. Rare great condors also make Patagonia their home, and although they do not primarily live in the desert, they are sometimes seen flying above it.

Desert Discovery

Vicuña fleece has been so valued for its softness that the ancient Inca people in Peru would shear the animals like sheep and weave garments for the Inca rulers. Anyone else caught wearing a garment spun from vicuña fleece was put to death. Even though the last Inca ruler was killed by the Spanish invaders in 1532, the fleece continued to be valuable. Today a pound of raw vicuña fleece sells for more than $225, making it the most expensive natural fiber in the world. This hasn't helped the vicuña population. It decreased from 2 million vicuña to a third of that by the 1960s. Poachers continued to hunt and kill many animals in the 1970s before conservationists stepped in to protect the animal from extinction. Thankfully, the population has rebounded. It has experienced an average of 17 percent growth each year since then.

Tuco-tuco

Absolute Atacama

Northern Chile is the location of our next South American desert. The Atacama Desert covers 140,000 square miles (363,000 sq km) in the foothills of the Andean Mountains, an area roughly the size of two-thirds of Italy and a little smaller than the state of California. This desert is growing every day by an area the size of 10 soccer fields.

This region often has less than a half an inch of rain a year. Atacama is on record as the driest desert in the world.

Atacama is unique in that it is a desert within a desert, meaning there is an area of this desert that is considered an "absolute desert." The only other region in the world that scientists consider an "absolute desert" is a part of the Sahara Desert of Africa. *Absolute deserts* are the most extreme deserts. How extreme? They receive less than half an inch of rain a year. How about an inch of rainfall in a period of 20 years? Now that's extreme!

Even though Atacama is the driest desert in the world, it is not very hot. The cool ocean current near the coast keeps the area mild with an average temperature of about 65°F (18.3°C). Visitors find Atacama cool and dry.

The People of Atacama

It is amazing that this extreme area can support any life, yet there are more than a million people who live in Atacama's coastal cities, mining towns, fishing villages, and even villages that have developed around desert oases. There are farmers who have developed vast irrigational systems to bring water to crops of tomatoes, olives, and cucumbers. The descendants of the Atacama natives herd llamas and alpacas. They have also developed ways to farm by using water from streams that form from melting snow in the higher elevations to irrigate their crops.

Make a Rain Stick

There is very little rain in this region of Chile, which is why the people of the desert wish and pray for rain every way they can. People in Chile make rain sticks out of cactus stems to serenade the gods in the hopes of being blessed with rain. To make their rain stick they first have to locate a cactus stem. They hollow out the stem and pound the thorns from another cactus into the stem in a spiraling pattern. They fill the stick with small pebbles, seeds, or beans. The ends of the stick are then capped and sealed. Last, they paint decorations on the outside of the stick. Here are directions to make your own rain stick to serenade the rain gods!

What You Need
- A grown-up to assist
- Wire cutters
- Chicken wire
- Cardboard wrapping paper tube
- Cardboard
- Pencil
- Scissors
- Clear packing tape
- Beans, rice, or small pebbles
- Markers

What You Do

1. Ask a grown-up to cut a length of chicken wire the length of your tube. Have the grown-up place the strip of chicken wire into the tube so that it is stretched out inside the tube from end to end.

2. Stand the cardboard tube up on the sheet of cardboard. Trace a circle slightly larger than the bottom of the tube with the pencil. Repeat this to create two circles.

3. Cut out both circles.

4. Use the clear packing tape to seal one end.

5. Add two handfuls of beans, rice, or pebbles to the tube.

6. Repeat step 4 to seal up the other end of the tube.

7. Use the markers to decorate the outside of your rain stick. To play your rain stick, tilt it slightly and let the beans, pebbles, or rice fall gently through the wire inside the stick to create the sound of rain in your tube.

Desert Discovery

Normally, clouds produce rain. But not in the Atacama Desert. There is a strange phenomenon in the desert caused by the Humboldt Current, named after German naturalist Baron Friedrich Heinrich Alexander Humboldt, who explored this region from 1799 to 1804. This current is similar to an ocean current, but instead of a river-like current running through the ocean, this current is a cold-air current. In some areas of the Atacama the cold air runs underneath layers of warmer air. This is just the opposite of normal conditions, and it causes a cloud layer over the desert. Usually clouds will produce rain, but this layer normally doesn't; instead, it hangs as gray mist or fog over the desert.

Acatama Salt Flat Experiment

Atacama has a series of salt basins that support virtually no vegetation. Because of this, there is little wildlife here. Try this experiment to see how these salt flats can develop.

What You Need

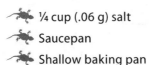

🦎 A grown-up to assist

🦎 1 cup (240 ml) water

🦎 ¼ cup (.06 g) salt

🦎 Saucepan

🦎 Shallow baking pan

What To Do

1. Place the water and salt in the saucepan. Ask a grown-up to heat it until the salt dissolves.

2. Pour the water into the baking pan and place it in a sunny window for two to three days.

3. What happens to the salt when the water evaporates into the air?

Check out the Desert Challenges section for an additional experiment.

Desert Lagoon Peeper

In all of this barrenness there is an astonishing natural lagoon that is 490 feet (150 m) deep. It is called the Chiu-Chiu Lagoon. Another lagoon, the Chaxa Lagoon, is also found in the desert. Among the many birds that call the lagoon home is a breeding colony of flamingos. Can you picture the pink flamingos standing beside the lagoon and surrounded by reddish-orange sands of the desert? What a sight! Here's how to create your own desert lagoon, complete with flamingos, like the Chaxa Lagoon in the Atacama Desert.

What You Need

- A grown-up to assist
- Shoebox with lid
- Scissors
- Orange tissue paper
- Pencil
- White craft glue
- Sand
- Card stock in blue and pink

What You Do

1. Poke a hole in the shoebox lid with the scissors, about ½ inch (1.3 cm) from the edge of the lid. Now cut a window in the lid, leaving the ½-inch (1.3-cm) margin from the edge.

2. Place the lid on the tissue paper and trace around it with a pencil. Cut out the completed rectangle and glue it to the underside of the lid to cover the window. Place the lid aside.

3. Using the scissors, cut a small peephole in the center of the small end of the shoebox.

4. Now it's time to create your desert. Place the lid gently on the box and take a peek inside through the peephole. The orange tissue paper will let just enough light in to make your desert appear to be orange. Start picturing your desert inside the box. Remove the lid and glue some sand and orange tissue paper to the inside of the box to cover the cardboard.

5. Cut three blue wave shapes to place in the middle for your desert lagoon. Be sure these are short enough so that

Desert Discovery

Flamingos use a system called *filter feeding* to eat tiny organisms, like diatoms. They suck in water through their bills and pass it through sieve-like plates in their mouths to filter out the tiny plants and animals that they eat. Their food is full of substances called *carotenoids* that turn the flamingos' feathers that lovely pink that we are so familiar with. The more carotenoids in their diet, the more pink they get. Feather color does, however, vary with flamingo species, ranging from pale pink to bright crimson.

you can still close the box lid. Fold down the bottom of the waves so that they will stand in your box after it is glued to the bottom.

6. Glue the first wave toward the front of your box, the second in the middle, and the third in the back. Look through the peephole while you position them so that you

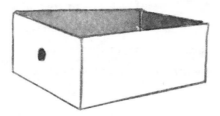
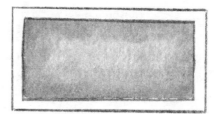

can make sure that you can see all three when they are glued in place.

7. After you have positioned your waves to form your lagoon, cut out your flamingos from the pink colored card stock. They can be glued around the lagoon.

8. Place the lid back onto the box when you have finished. Take a peek through the peephole. How does your desert lagoon look?

Desert Discovery

Atacama is very dry. How dry is it, you ask? Well, it is so dry that people have actually developed fog catchers to catch the moisture from the fog to help provide a water source for nearby towns. The fog catchers are made of screens that trap or catch the fog, which then drips down into pipes that take the water to the towns.

Atacama Mars-Scapes

Scientists know that the planet Mars is very cold and very dry. They have been studying the effects of cold on people for a very long time, but they have not learned much about the effects of such a dry environment on people. To learn more about this, scientists have begun to look at Atacama, since it is perhaps the driest place on earth. They are studying how life can exist in the desert with very little water. Look up information on Mars in the library or on the Internet and see if you can find any other similarities between Atacama and the red planet. Are there many differences?

Journey to the Sahara and Beyond

Now that we have explored the deserts of the Americas, it's time to fly to the continent of Africa and explore the deserts there. So pack up your things and head to the airport for the journey to Africa and the great Sahara Desert.

JOURNEY TO THE SAHARA, NAMIB, KALAHARI, AND NEGEV

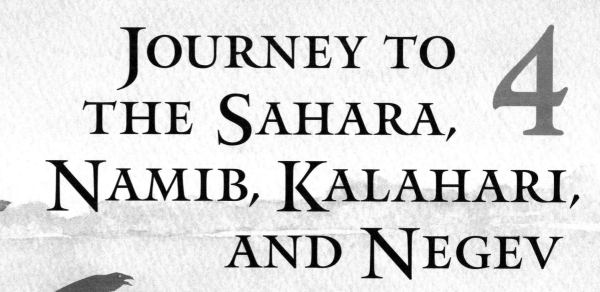

4

The continent of Africa has just about every type of environment. There are treeless grasslands, savannahs with scattered trees and wild grasses, layered rainforests with lush vegetation, and dry deserts. The Sahara Desert is probably one of the most well-known deserts in the world, and it will be our first stop on our expedition to the deserts of Africa. But we can't leave Africa without journeying to the others—the Namib, the Kalahari, and the Negev. To begin, look at a globe and see if you can find the Sahara Desert on the continent of Africa.

The Journey Begins in the Sahara

The Sahara is the world's largest desert, stretching over 3.5 million square miles (9.1 million sq km), and is covered by mountains 10,000 feet (3,048 m) high, gravel plains, salt flats, rocky areas, and huge areas of dunes. The Sahara is bordered on the west by the Atlantic Ocean, on the east by the Red Sea and Egypt, on the north by the Mediterranean Sea and the Atlas Mountains, and on the south by the Sudan and the Niger River Valley. There are fewer than 2 million people living in this desert, most of them nomads, like the Tuareg people, who historically bred and traded camels. With all that sand it is hard to imagine that the Sahara also boasts a lake the size of the state of New Jersey.

Stuffed Dates

Dates, which are high in nutritional value, are a staple food in the desert oases of the southern area of Morocco, a country in the Sahara Desert. They are low in fat and high in fiber, and are a good source of minerals. Dates also provide calcium and protein. Muslims, who practice fasting, or abstaining from food, at certain times of the year for religious reasons, usually break their fast by eating dates.

Dates grow on trees called date palms. They need plenty of water, which is why they grow only in the areas of desert oases, where the groundwater supplies are the most plentiful. They take a full year to mature before they can be harvested. They are the sweetest and plumpest when the temperature is the hottest. The Moroccans say that the date palms like to "have their heads in fire and their feet in water," which means they grow best when it is hot and their roots have a lot of moisture. Make this delicious Moroccan treat with dates to share with your friends.

What You Need

- A grown-up to assist
- 1-pound package of pitted dates
- ½ cup (100 ml) honey
- Saucepan
- Mixing bowl
- ½ cup (0.1 g) finely chopped almonds
- Wooden spoon
- Sugar, coconut, or toasted sesame seeds

What You Do

1. Ask a grown-up to slice the pitted dates open so it will be easier for you to stuff them.

2. Place the honey in the saucepan and heat on a low flame until it is foamy, about 8 minutes. Remove from the heat.

3. Pour the honey in the mixing bowl and add the almonds. Let the mixture cool until it thickens.

4. Spoon a little bit of the mixture into your hand, then roll it in sugar, coconut, or sesame seeds.

5. Carefully stuff each date with the mixture. Serve your candies to your friends and family. Yum!

Grow Your Own Date Palm

If you can find dates in the supermarket that still have their pits, you can save the pits to grow your own date palm. Here's how.

What You Need

- Dates with pits
- Small terra-cotta planter
- Potting soil
- Water
- Clear plastic wrap
- Rubber band
- Sand

What You Do

1. Use your fingers to open up the date and remove the pit from the date.

2. Rinse the pit in the sink.

3. Fill the planter with the potting soil and place the pit on top of the soil.

4. Sprinkle the soil and pit with water.

5. Cover the planter with clear plastic wrap and secure with a rubber band. Place it in a sunny window.

6. After a week or so you will see a root growing from your pit. At that point, mix in some sand to your soil so that you have about 40 percent sand and 60 percent soil. Turn your pit so that the root is pointed down into the soil. Cover the root completely with the soil mixture.

7. Water and cover again with plastic wrap. When you see a sprout grow out of the date seed, remove the plastic wrap. Water your plant when the soil feels dry. Do not let the pit sit in water.

The Lily of the Desert

Have you ever gotten a sunburn and had someone spread cool aloe vera gel on top of it to relieve the heat? As long ago as 1500 B.C. Ancient Egyptians were using the gel inside the leaves of the aloe vera plant to relieve burns and other ailments. Aloe vera gel from the plant, a native to the African desert, has wonderful healing properties, and that is why it is still so popular today. In addition to providing sunburn relief, it is also used to aid digestion and blood circulation, and to soothe ulcers. Many people keep an aloe plant in their kitchen just in case they get a burn while they're cooking. If you accidentally burn yourself you can break off a piece of the aloe plant and let the clear gel flow over the burn.

Visit a health food or drug store and see how many products you can find that have aloe listed as one of the ingredients.

Desert Discovery
You've probably seen pictures of both one-humped camels and two-humped camels. As we have seen, the one-humped, or dromedary, camels are found in Africa. Two-humped camels, called Bactrians, are found in the Gobi Desert of Asia.

Camel Countdown

The one-humped, or dromedary, camel lives in herds in the deserts of Africa. These camels are well adapted to the harsh environment of the desert. Their nostrils can squeeze to such a narrow slit that airborne sand in sandstorms cannot penetrate, yet they can still breathe. Their eyes have long eyelashes that provide protection from blowing sand. Their eyelids allow enough light to pass through them so that they can shut their eyes during a sandstorm and enough light will still pass through them to allow the camel to see where it's walking. Camels also have especially wide foot pads that help them balance as they walk on the loose, moving sand.

So what about that big hump on the its back? Does it really hold water? Well, it really doesn't store water. It actually stores fat. Camels have other ways of getting and retaining water in the desert. First of all, camels don't sweat like many other animals. They are able to raise and lower their body temperatures so that the temperature of the desert air is not much different than their own body temperatures, which reduces the need to sweat. This allows camels to hold more fluids in their bodies. Like some other desert animals, they don't urinate much, either. Their noses are designed so that the moisture in their breath is absorbed by their nose before it even hits the outside air. When camels finally do get a chance to drink some water, they really fill themselves up. They can drink as much as 30 gallons (114 l) of water at one time, filling their belly until it bulges. Can you imagine drinking that much of anything at one time?

How else can animals adapt to their surroundings? Let's take a look at some other animals to see how their bodies have adapted to their habitats.

Dromedary camel

What You Need

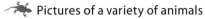 Pictures of a variety of animals

What You Do

1. Look at a picture of a camel and count the number of different body parts that help it live in the desert. Does it have feet that help it walk on sand? Eyes that have protective lashes or lids to keep the sand and wind out? What color is the fur of a camel? How might this be helpful?

2. Now look at a picture of another desert animal that lives in the Sahara Desert, such as the fennec fox. What color is the animal? Does its color blend in with its surroundings? Why do you think it has such large ears? The fox has very large black eyes that help it see at night. Do you think it's nocturnal? Count the different parts of the animal's body that help it live in the desert.

3. Compare these two animals to two animals that live in your region. For example, look at a white-tailed deer and a red fox. How do these animals differ from the animals that live in the desert? Are there lizards where you live? Why do you suppose lizards either live or don't live in your area?

Fennec fox

Red fox

Why Camels Make Faces: An Egyptian Legend

Camels are known to make all sorts of faces. Some make the camel look disgusted or annoyed. Muslims have an explanation for the many faces camels make. They believe that the prophet Mohammed once told the secret of all secrets to the camel. What was this secret he told the camel? Muslims who practice the religion of Islam believe that Allah (God) has 99 known names, but there is one more. That 100th name is hidden. The 99 names are just descriptions for Allah, but it is believed that they do not tell us the true identity of Allah. The 100th is the name that might tell us the true identity. Muslims believe that Mohammed told the camel the 100th name of Allah. They also believe that the camel now roams the desert and makes faces in disgust at every person he sees who does not know the 100th name of Allah.

People of the Veil

The Tuaregs (TWAH-regs) are nomads who live in the Sahara and travel by camel. They are known as "people of the veil" because of the turbans and layers of clothing they wear to protect them from the harsh desert environment. They are descended from ancient Berber tribes of North Africa and were historically camel breeders and traders. Many years ago they ruled the trade routes through the Sahara, trading in salt and bringing gold, silver, and ivory to the north. They are now seminomadic, meaning they do not roam as much as their ancestors. They live in four countries in Africa: Libya, Algeria, Mauritania, and Mali. Have you ever heard of Timbuktu? Timbuktu was founded in A.D. 1100 by the Tuaregs as a seasonal camp, meaning they would only stay there for a season rather than permanently. Timbuktu passed through many different rulers over the centuries, including Muslim scholars, the French, and Moroccans. It is now a city in the African nation of Mali. There are still some salt caravans, carrying salt for trade, that pass through the city, but there is no longer the amount of Sahara trading that once existed.

Exploring the Sahara

While the Tuaregs were at home in the Sahara, explorers came from Europe to learn more about this vast desert. Rene Caillie (run-A kay-A), a Frenchman, heard tales of the splendor and riches of Timbuktu,

then spent eleven years planning his journey there. He left on his trek in 1827 disguised as an Arab trader. Many claim that he was the first European to visit Timbuktu, cross the Sahara, and live to tell of his adventure. He stayed in Timbuktu for two weeks before joining a caravan and crossing the Sahara. He must have been quite disappointed to find out that the city of Timbuktu was not made of gold as he believed. Instead he found quicksand and what he called "ill-looking houses." He completed his expedition the next year when he reached Tangier. There he boarded a ship for his voyage back to France.

Oasis in the Desert

An *oasis* is a place in the desert that has water and is therefore able to support plants and other wildlife. The world's largest oasis, the Nile valley, runs through 1,600 miles (2,575 km) of absolute desert. It is perhaps best known for one of history's greatest civilizations, ancient Egypt. This civilization began about 5,000 years ago and continued to prosper for about 3,000 years. The desert helped shape ancient Egyptian society by making it almost untouchable. The deserts that surrounded Egypt were too difficult for any attackers to cross. Much of what we know about this great civilization was uncovered from the desert sands that buried the artifacts and pyramids long ago. Even today discoveries are being made, such as the recent discovery of mummies that may be buried in the lost grave of Egyptian Queen Nefertiti. Along with the discoveries, archeologists and scientists are still searching for information. Visit a museum to see some of the artifacts of ancient Egypt that have been discovered in the pyramids and sands of Egypt.

Desert Discovery

The Great Sphinx, a sandstone monument, is a creature that has a head of a woman and the body of a lion. The word *sphinx* means "strangler" in Greek and describes a creature that the Greeks described as having the head of a woman, the body of a lion, and the wings of a bird. Why do you think the Egyptians built such a monument, carved from rock from the desert, with a lion's body? That answer brings us to the desert. The Egyptians feared the desert. It was a place of great heat and very cold nights. It was a place without water and with wild animals, nomads, and other feared people. The Egyptians even believed that there were demons living in the desert. Lions roamed the edges of the desert, and the Egyptians believed that they were the "guardians of the horizon." In fact, it is said that the Egyptian ruler Ramses II, who ruled from 1279 to 1213 B.C., even had a pet lion that went into battle with him and slept in his tent. So why not build such a magnificent monument with a lion's body?

The Namib Desert

The Namib Desert covers 52,000 square miles (135,000 sq km) in the country of Namibia on the coast of southwestern Africa. It stretches for 1,200 miles (1,920 km) along the coast. In the ancient Nama language of the region, *Namib* means vast, and the desert certainly is. It is home to the highest sand dunes in the world and, like so many of the other deserts, it has spectacular scenery. It is reported that the coast of the desert holds the world's greatest source of gemstones.

Namib Desert Dwellers

What creatures are able to live in such an extreme desert environment? Take the tenebrionid (tuh-NEB-ree-uh-nud) beetle. It is able to survive by raising its back end into the fog of the desert. Tiny droplets of water collect on it and allow the beetle a precious drink of water. The web-footed gecko, a lizard with a short body, a big head, and suction pads that look like balls on its feet, also takes advantage of the fog for its morning drink. The gecko has a long tongue that enables it to lick the droplets from its head. It spends the day burrowed in the sand, waiting for the cool night so it can move around again and hunt for insects. The sidewinding viper also licks the collected water droplets from its body after the morning fog.

Not all animals are quiet during the day. Many beetles, such as the dung beetle, are active throughout the day. They spend the day searching for leaves and seeds, then burrow into the sand as night comes to stay warm.

Tenebrionid beetle

Desert Discovery

The Egyptians worshipped many gods and goddesses. Seth was a god that the Egyptians associated with the desert. Egyptians both feared the desert, because of its harsh and unforgiving environment, and valued it, because it was rich in resources that the Egyptians valued, such as gold, amethyst, and turquoise.

Sandbox Sand Dunes

The dunes in the desert can reach enormous heights and form many different patterns. They can also be very small and show only ripples. Unlike other areas, the desert offers no obstructions to the wind that blows freely over the sands causing these patterns. The shapes of these dunes define the types of winds that form them. For example, the very stable star dunes are formed from wind that blows from all directions, whereas the barchan dunes, which are crescent shaped, form as a result of one-directional wind that blows the sand more steadily over the dune's low tips than over its center. Longitudinal dunes result when strong one-way winds blow over sand that is made up of both coarse and fine sand, cutting long troughs parallel with the wind's path. Last, transverse dunes are the result of more moderate winds that blow over

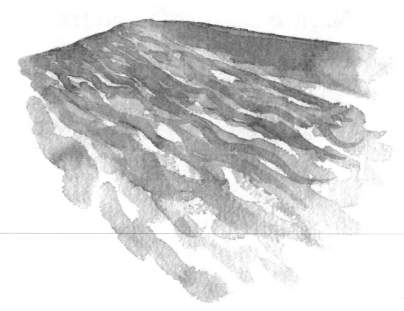

lighter, finer sand. The blowing air tumbles and causes ridges. Here's how to make some of these patterns in a smaller desert—your sandbox.

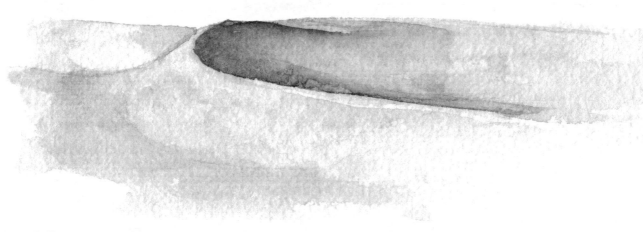

The Kalahari

The Kalahari Desert, in southwestern Africa, covers 200,000 square miles (520,000 sq km) and is covered by sand dunes and gravel plains. There are acacia trees, aloe plants, and baobab trees. Along with gerbils and gazelles, you'll also find jackals and hyenas.

Hyenas are known for their laugh. It is not really a laugh like a human laugh. The hyena's laugh is part of its method of communication. Hyenas communicate with each other by using a variety of calls, some of which sound like laughing or giggling.

What You Need

 Sandbox

 Pictures of dunes

 Straws

What You Do

1. Smooth out the sand in your sandbox with your hand.

2. Use your straw to blow the sand in different directions. Can you create any of the patterns described?

3. Ask a friend to help create more wind for your sandbox. Try blowing the sand in the same direction and see what shape it forms, then try blowing the sand from different directions. What types of dunes did you create?

More About the Baobab

The baobab tree is perhaps one of the most recognizable trees on the planet. In fact, if you have visited Disney's Animal Kingdom, you have undoubtedly seen the man-made baobab tree that is the center attraction of the park. Like the tree at the park, baobab trees are very large, and they dominate their surroundings. They reach heights of 82 feet (25 m) and can have a trunk diameter of more than 32.8 feet (10 m). It is believed that they can live to be over 1,000 years old. The baobab tree's name is derived from the Egyptian name for the tree, *buhobab*. Famed explorer Dr. David

Livingstone spoke about the tree as a "giant upturned carrot." Read this African legend about the baobab tree and then see if you can make up your own.

A long, long time ago when the desert was young, there lived a baobab tree. It was a beautiful tree with long sweeping branches that shaded the animals from the strong desert sun. But the baobab tree was not happy. Every day the baobab tree would sweep her branches up into the blue sky and say to the Great Spirit, "Great Spirit, am I not beautiful?"

Every day the Great Spirit would look down on the baobab and her sweeping branches and say, "Yes, dear, Baobab, you are very beautiful."

This did not satisfy the baobab, who would then exclaim, "Great Spirit, I want to be more beautiful. I want to be the most beautiful tree in all the world."

The Great Spirit would sigh, and a warm wind would blow down upon the desert, and all its creatures and the desert would become even hotter.

The animals that sat in the shade of the baobab would also sigh, for they needed the shade and not the warm wind that continued to blow each day from the Great Spirit.

This went on for many days and then many months. The Great Spirit was growing weary of the baobab's desire to be the most beautiful tree in the world. After all, each tree is beautiful, is it not? There is not one tree more pretty than another in the eyes of the Great Spirit.

The baobab was still not satisfied and asked yet again the same question, "Great Spirit, am I not beautiful?"

The Great Spirit looked down again on the baobab and her sweeping branches and said, "Yes, dear, Baobab, you are very beautiful."

Unsatisfied, the baobab again exclaimed, "Great Spirit, I want to be more beautiful. I want to be the most beautiful tree in all the world."

This time the Great Spirit did not sigh. The Great Spirit, weary from the baobab's complaints, picked up the baobab, turned her over, and placed her back in the desert soil so that her roots stuck up into the sky and she could no longer be heard. This certainly quieted the baobab, who then only grew leaves once a year.

The baobab's roots continue to climb toward the sky to this day. Do you think they are reaching for the Great Spirit to turn the tree back over again? I do.

Create a Desert Creature

Here's your chance to create your own creature to live in the African desert.

What You Need
 Markers

Paper

What You Do

1. Think about all the different creatures that live in the desert, and then invent your own creature to live in an African desert. Will it be a reptile, insect, bird, or mammal?

2. Decide if your creature will be nocturnal (active at night) or *diurnal* (active in the daytime). Will it burrow in the sand, or find a place above the ground to live?

3. What kind of feet will it have? Will it have claws to climb, or claws to dig? Will it have wide feet or tiny feet? What color is your creature?

4. Draw a picture of your creature. Color your new desert creature as it would be seen in the desert.

5. Last, give your creature a name.

6. For more fun, write a story about a day in the life of your creature. Include all the activities that fill its waking hours, from dawn to dusk, or from dusk to dawn.

The Sahel

Sahel is an Arabic term for the narrow strip of land that separates desert from savanna. It comes from the Arabic word meaning "edge" or "border." This narrow area is shrinking at an alarming rate. This is caused primarily by animals grazing on the vegetation there and by people cutting down bushes and trees for firewood to heat their homes from the bitter cold of the desert at night. When the vegetation disappears, the topsoil blows away, leaving only rocky land where crops cannot grow. You'll learn more about this process of desertification in chapter 9.

On the Other Side: Plants Fight Back

Satellite photos have spotted an increase in vegetation, which is edging out sand dunes in part of the African deserts, from Mauritania to Eritrea. This area once suffered from desertification. Increased rainfall and better farming techniques have turned this around. You'll learn more about this, too, in chapter 9.

Onward

Is the heat of the African deserts taking a toll on you yet? Imagine how the early explorers felt without the comforts that are available to us now. Well, it's time to leave these dry sands behind and head a bit north to the desert regions of Asia. Do you think it will be cooler? Let's hope so!

The Red and Black Deserts of Asia 5

Leaving the deserts of Africa, we now fly to Asia, where we'll discover singing sands and our own common rodent, the gerbil. Look at a globe and find Asia. Asia is the largest continent on the planet. Because its desert lands are on the other side of the high peaks of the Himalayan Mountains, humidity from the Indian Ocean never has a chance to reach them. Like the deserts of North America, they are not near other bodies of water. This situation causes the deserts of Asia to experience extreme weather conditions—very cold winters and very hot summers—both with little moisture.

Locating the Deserts

Most of the deserts in this region have unfamiliar names, like Kara Kum, Thar, and Taklimakan, but you may have heard of the Gobi, which is a little more well known than the other deserts. The Gobi is the largest, covering 500,000 square miles (1,300,000 sq km) in the countries of China and Mongolia. Let's take a look at where the other deserts in this region are located. The Taklimakan covers about 105,000 square miles (269,000 sq km) in the Sinkiang Province of western China. The Thar covers a little more area, about 175,000 square miles (449,000 sq km), and is found in western India and Pakistan. The Kara Kum covers 135,000 square miles (346,000 sq km) in the country of Turkmenistan.

Sand Study

In many deserts, sand shapes the landscape we see. The sand carried by rushing streams that wear down rock in the desert forms canyons and other land formations. The sand is also carried by the wind and acts like a sandblaster to shape some of the rocky landscapes we see.

You've probably visited a beach and felt the sand underneath your toes. You may have even looked at it closely with a magnifying glass and found tiny bits of shell, coral, or rock in your sample. The sand of the deserts is not much different. It is also made up of tiny grains of minerals and rocks, but it might be a bit difficult to see parts of shells in a desert sand sample that is so far from the ocean. Even so, you might find tiny crystals of quartz and other minerals that are in both beach and desert sand. These minerals, rocks, and other matter in the sand create the color of the sand.

The Kara Kum Desert is named after the black sand there. *Kara Kum* actually translates to "black sands" in the Turkmen language. Another desert area in central Asia, called Kyzylkum, has red sands. What do you think you would find if you looked at sand from a desert in your country? Let's see.

What You Need
 Desert sand
Paper
Magnifying glass

What You Do

1. Spread some desert sand out on a piece of paper. What color is it?

2. Examine your sample with the magnifying glass. Do you see any other colors now that you are looking at the sample up close?

3. See if you can identify different particles that make up your sand sample.

4. Most desert sand is made up of quartz minerals. See if you can find out what other minerals are found in sand. For an extra challenge, take a look at the Desert Challenges section.

Desert Explorers

The deserts of this region were formed 22 million years ago and have been explored by many people in their vast history. In the 13th century the deserts were crossed by explorers, who were not as concerned with mapping or history as they were with silks and other treasures they hoped to find there.

Taklimakan was crossed in the 13th century by the explorer Marco Polo (1254–1324). He spent two years on his journey from Venice, Italy, to the eastern coast of China. Later, he claimed to have been spooked by noises in the desert that sounded like "many instruments sounding." Do you think it was the sound of the wind blowing through the dune fields, or desert spirits, as Polo believed?

In the same century, Genghis Khan crossed the Gobi Desert. Genghis Khan was a Mongolian, born in the year 1162. At birth he was named Temujin, but when he united many Mongolian warring tribes he was given the name of Genghis Khan, meaning "universal ruler." During his life he conquered most of China and Mongolia, forming one of the greatest empires the world has ever known. His desert crossing was just one branch of his journey to conquer Asia.

Desert Discovery

You might find that the sand you walk on at the beach makes a sound when you step down on it. The dry sands in the deserts make even more noises. They squeak, rumble, and sometimes sound as if they even roar. You might even hear people refer to some areas as having "singing sands" or "booming sands." Why? Well, these sounds are created when piles of sun-baked sand break up and roll down the face of a dune. When scientists look at the sands from these noisy areas of deserts they have found that the sand is more polished than in other areas.

Mongolian Hot Pot

Have you ever eaten fondue? Perhaps you have a fondue pot that you melt chocolate in for dipping fruit. Well, a Mongolian hot pot is like a Chinese fondue.

Traditionally the hot pot is a brass pot with a wide outer rim, a chimney in the center, and a charcoal burner underneath. It is filled with water and heated until the water boils. The community members sharing the pot dip slices of raw meat and vegetables in the water, which cook very quickly. They then dip their cooked food in a sesame sauce and eat it. Over time, the flavors of the foods that are dipped into the boiling water help create a rich broth that further flavors the food.

Temperatures in the Gobi desert vary tremendously. They can range from 104°F (40°C) in the summer to −40°F (−40°C) in the winter. The Mongolian hot pot is a food that is prepared during those cold win-

ters. By the 18th century, it had become a favorite winter meal in most of China, and it still remains a favorite today. What do you eat when it's really cold out? Next winter, try this recipe and see if it warms you up!

What You Need

- A grown-up to assist
- Vegetable broth (2 14-ounce (1 liter) cans or enough to fill your pot)
- Fondue pot
- Ginger (4 slices of fresh or a sprinkle of powdered)
- ⅜ teaspoon (15 ml) chopped garlic
- Mixing bowl
- ½ cup (100 ml) peanut butter
- 1½ teaspoons (7.5 ml) soy sauce
- 1 tablespoon (15 ml) water
- Small individual bowls for sauce
- Thinly sliced, bite-sized pieces of chicken or beef
- Chopped vegetables including Chinese cabbage, mushrooms, and any other vegetables you like
- Fondue skewers

What You Do

1. Add the vegetable broth to the fondue pot. Ask a grown-up to help you. Heat the broth according to the directions of your pot, bringing it to a boil. If your pot does not heat the water to boiling, heat the broth on the stove and add it to the pot after it boils.

2. Add the ginger and ⅓ of the garlic to the broth.

3. Prepare the dipping sauce. In a mixing bowl, mix together the peanut butter, soy sauce, water and ¼ teaspoon garlic. Pour the sauce into individual small bowls for everyone to use during the meal.

4. Place the vegetables and meats on plates around the pot so that everyone can reach them during the meal.

5. When you are ready to eat, allow everyone room to reach all the foods, the sauce, and the hot pot. Take turns skewering a piece of food and cooking it in the pot. Make sure the meat or vegetable is cooked before you eat it. Dip it into the sauce and taste.

Gerbil Study

Many of the small burrowing animals found in deserts have become household pets. But where do they come from? The animals you see in the pet stores are not actually from the desert, but are bred in captivity. This means that they are not taken out of the wild. In fact, the gerbil you buy in the pet store is many generations removed from its ancestors in the desert. Let's take a look at where the gerbil's relatives are found.

Gerbils are commonly found in the deserts of Asia, the Middle East, and Africa. Like many other desert mammals, they are *nocturnal*, meaning they are active at night and sleep during the day. You might already know this if you have a gerbil in your house. In the desert they eat mostly grains, seeds, and roots. They drink very little water and are able to get most of the water they need from the seeds they eat. Gerbils often bring back food to their burrows to eat later. Most gerbils in America are the descendants of nine Mongolian gerbils that were brought here in 1954 by Dr. Victor Schwentker for research.

Kangaroo rats look very much like gerbils and are commonly found in the deserts of the United States; however, they are a bit larger than gerbils. Kangaroo rats range from about 9 to 16 inches (22.86 cm to

Gerbils

40.64 cm) long, not including their tails. Gerbils are only about 3 to 7 inches (7.6 to 17.8 cm) long, not including their tails.

Let's study a gerbil to see how it might live in the desert.

What You Need

- Gerbils (visit a pet shop that sells gerbils)
- Pad of paper
- Pencil

What You Do

1. Here's a list of questions to ask yourself when you set out to study gerbils at a pet store. Write these down on your pad of paper. Where do the gerbils sleep? What do they eat? Are they asleep during your visit or active? Are they digging in their bedding? Where do they store their food? How often do their cages need to be cleaned? How does this compare with other rodents, such as hamsters and mice, in the pet store? Is it less often or more often? Add some questions of your own.

2. Visit the pet store with your pad of paper filled with questions. See if you can find answers to all of your questions. You might have to ask someone who works at the store.

3. Look at the answers to the questions and see how pet-store gerbils' behaviors compare to that of gerbils in their natural desert environment. Did you find piles of food stored in other areas of their tank or cage, just as you would

find in a burrow in the wild? Did you find many sleeping in the daytime, as they would in the desert? Did you find that their tank or cage doesn't need to be cleaned as often as that of some other rodents that drink much more water and urinate more often in their cage?

4. Close your eyes. Can you imagine a little gerbil living in the desert? How will it behave in one 24-hour period?

Animals of the Asian Deserts

Many other creatures call the Asian deserts home. Some you have probably never heard of, such as

Przewalski's (shuh-VALL-skis) horse, or *takhi* in Mongolian, a small horse that lives in the Gobi desert. The *takhi* is the last true wild horse in the world. Its coat is sandy colored, but it grows darker and thicker in the colder months. Twenty thousand years ago the *takhi* roamed across Europe and Asia, but after the Ice Age the climate changed and the *takhi* began to be hunted by humans. In Asia the nomadic herds competed with the wild horses. By the late 1960s the *takhi* disappeared from the desert. Only a small population kept in zoos remained. Thanks to many zoos and other organizations, the *takhi* are now being reintroduced to their native environment. Their numbers have now reached 1,200.

The small rodent called the *jerboa* (jur-BO-uh) is one of those small mammals that live nocturnally in the desert. Even though they are very small, they can jump 10 feet. Pretty incredible, huh? The Gobi is also home to some larger mammals, including the Asiatic ibex, the Gobi bear, and the wild, two-humped,

Bactrian camel. Perhaps you have been lucky enough to see a snow leopard in a zoo. Well, snow leopards also make their home in the Gobi. They are adapted to this region's rocky terrain and snowy peaks. This beautiful, endangered member of the cat family makes its home in the mountain ridges of the Mongolian Gobi region. Poaching for their beautiful fur has caused a decline in the population of these great animals, but there are many conservation groups working to protect them.

Desert Discovery

Snow leopards have been hunted nearly to extinction. According to statistics, there are only about 2,500 adult leopards left in the wild. That's too few for conservationists.

The Corral Improvement Project is a collaboration between the Snow Leopard Conservancy and The Mountain Institute to help protect snow leopards from being killed by herders who hunt down snow leopards that have attacked their herds. The project has established corrals to protect the herds from the snow leopards. Since the corrals' completion there have been no snow leopard attacks on the livestock. The project has been very successful.

Snow leopard

Marmot in the Middle Game

Snow leopards feed on many different animals, from large mammals—such as the wild mountain goat and the ibex, which can be three times their own weight—to much smaller rodents, such as marmots that resemble woodchucks or gophers. Here's a predator–prey game about snow leopards and marmots that you can play outside with your friends.

Marmot

What You Need

🦎 8 or more friends

🦎 Wide-open play area

What You Do

1. Pick two friends to be marmots and two friends to be snow leopards.

2. Have everyone else makes a circle around the marmots to keep the leopards out.

3. The snow leopards try to break the circle and tag a marmot. If they do, then the tagged marmot is out, and he or she picks someone else to be a marmot in the middle.

The Tale of Day and Night from Mongolia

This folktale comes from Mongolia. As in many other folktales around the world, the animal in this tale takes the form of a human being. This story is a *pourquoi* tale, a folktale that is designed to explain something. (Did you know that *pourquoi* is the French word for "why"?) In this case, it explains why there is day and night.

Long ago, when the marmot walked the earth as a man, there were seven suns that shined all day and all night. The seven suns sent rays down upon the earth, causing the earth to dry. Famine and hardship came to the people of the land. It was then that the man shot arrows into the suns, bringing six of them down. The seventh sun escaped the arrows by circling the earth. The sun still circles the earth, even after the man became a marmot. That is why we now have days with light and nights without. It is also said that the marmot still retains a little bit of the flesh from man, and that is why his meat can never be eaten.

Marmots are prone to certain diseases, such as the plague. Perhaps this is why people did not hunt them years ago. Today Mongolians hunt marmots for meat, fur, and oil.

valleys, and hillsides. Forests of these shrubs protect the sands from erosion and movement. *Erosion* occurs when there is nothing holding the soil in place and it slowly wears away. In some cases it washes away or blows away. People in this region often use the wood from the shrubs for firewood, which is harmful to the ecosystem because there are so few other plants to hold onto the soil. It is important for the people of this region to search out alternative fuel sources. Can you think of any alternatives?

The Saxaul

This woody shrub plays a very important part in the desert community of this region. Saxaul grow between 6 and 12 feet (1.8 m and 3.6 m) in moving soils, rocky

Heading Down Under

Well, it's time to leave Asia and fly back across the equator to Australia, the great southern land more commonly called the "land down under."

DESERTS 6 DOWN UNDER

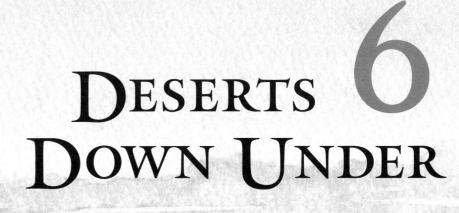

Welcome to the land down under. Australia is the only country to inhabit a whole continent. It is the sixth largest nation in the world. The country's original inhabitants, the aborigines, have origins dating back to the last Ice Age. More recently, in 1787, Great Britain sent convicts to the colony of Australia to solve overcrowding in its prisons. The discovery of gold in the 1850s brought many more people to Australia.

Although much of Australia is semiarid to arid deserts, Australia also has lush rainforests. The deserts, however, are our destination.

61

They are separated from the more fertile coastal area by the Great Dividing Range, a group of mountains that run north and south down the eastern seaboard. There are five deserts to explore: the coastal Great Sandy, the interior Gibson, the Great Victoria in southwestern Australia, and the Tanami and Simpson in the interior Northern Territory of Australia. Together these deserts make up the area known as the outback. It is also known as the heart of Australia. Let's begin our journey and find out why.

Strange and Mysterious Formations

The Olgas are not a pop band from down under. They're a group of about 30 dome-shaped peaks that lie west of Ayers Rock in Australia's Northern Territory. They are the eroded remains of a mountain range that is now long gone from this region. The Olgas rose above the sea that was once there about 500 million years ago. The aborigines have used them as a source of fresh water and shelter for thousands of years. In fact, there are cave paintings created by these early people in the caves underneath the Olgas that can still be seen today. The aboriginal people call the area *Kata Tjuta*, or "many heads."

Famous Ayers Rock

Ayers Rock, called *Uluru* by native aboriginal people, is a giant sandstone *monolith*, or giant block of stone. It was shaped by the constant wind and blowing sand 500 million years ago. The rock rises 1,142 feet (348 m) above the surrounding plain and stretches for 5 miles (8 km) around its base. It is because it rises up from a flat plain that Ayers Rock, like the Olgas, is known as an *inselberg*, or an island mountain. Many people visit the area to view the colors of the rock throughout the day. The rock varies from a bright orange to a dark crimson, with many shades in between, depending on the angle of the sun. This strange phenomenon is caused by the sun shining on different stones within the entire rock of the monolith.

People of the Desert

The Australian aborigines are the native people who have made the outback their home for thousands of years. When ocean explorer Captain James Cook landed in Australia in the year 1770 there were about 300,000 aborigines living in roughly 500 tribes or clans. Colonization by the British greatly interrupted the lives of the aborigines. They not only lost their hunting grounds and their watering holes, but they acquired diseases they could not fight. Their numbers dropped. Today, due in part to better medicines and land-rights legislation, their population has increased to more than 380,000.

One tribe, the Bindibu, remained unseen by explorers until an expedition in 1957 found them. This group lived very close to the way that Stone Age tribes lived. They were nomadic hunters and food gatherers without any permanent homes or crops to sustain them. Although there were kangaroos nearby, there were no animals that possessed hair or wool satisfactory for weaving, so this tribe did not dress in the flowing garments of other desert people. Instead, they wore nothing. Their dark skin contains natural pigments that provide them protection from the harsh rays of the sun, therefore preventing them from getting sunburned, as lighter-skinned people would.

Dreamtime Painting

The *dreamtime* is the beginning of knowledge for the aboriginal people. It is believed that the earth was flat in the dreamtime. It was a dark and silent time for the earth. Then the supernatural Ancestor Beings broke through the earth from below with great force. It was then that the sun also rose and light shone down upon the land for the first time. The Ancestors then created everything on earth. When they grew tired of all they had done, they went back into the earth.

Dreamtime stories are Australian aboriginal tales about the time of creation. They describe how things came to be, where to find food, and how to behave. There are many stories. Dreamtime paintings are created to tell some of those stories or are inspired by those stories. Dreamtime paintings are among the old-est paintings in the world. The early paintings of 50,000 to 70,000 years ago were painted in dots. They incorporated history, mythology, geography, and the culture of the ancient people who painted them. Here's how to make your own dreamtime painting.

What You Need

- Brown paper
- Pencil
- Paint cups
- Tempera paint, primary colors
- Paintbrush
- Cotton swabs

What You Do

1. Decide what dreamtime image you want to paint. Consider the Australian desert and the animals that live there for your painting. Draw your image on the brown paper with the pencil.

2. Fill the paint cups with tempera paints. Mix the paints together in other cups to create additional colors.

3. Outline your image with your paintbrush in the color of paint you choose. Use the cotton swabs to fill in your work. Keep in mind that dreamtime paintings are usually created with dots and some lines.

4. Look at some dreamtime stories listed in the Desert Resources section. Pick one and create a dreamtime painting of that tale.

Rolla-Mano and the Evening Star: A Dreamtime Story

The aborigines traveled between the Australian deserts and the ocean. Their nights were filled with starry skies. This dreamtime tale tells how some of those stars came to be.

In the dreamtime, many ages ago, Rolla-Mano ruled the kingdom of the sea. His domain was filled with glistening pearls, pink coral, and white sea foam. In this strange land of green shadows and filtered rays of sunlight were trees of brown sea kelp and patches of feathery sea grass. Here Rolla-Mano ruled over the brightly colored fish, dark, grey sharks, and quick-moving crabs.

Close to the shore was a lonely mangrove swamp where Rolla-Mano often went to fish for his dinner. One day, as he was cooking some of his catch over an open fire, he noticed two beautiful girls through the reeds. Their voices mingled with the soft breezes of the night, intoxicating Rolla-Mano. He became determined to capture them and bring them to his watery kingdom.

Hiding behind the branches of a mangrove tree, he readied his net. When the girls came a bit closer, Rolla-Mano threw his net over them. One girl escaped and dove quickly into the shimmering waters. Rolla-Mano became so enraged that he ran after the girl with a burning stick from his fire. As the stick touched the water the sparks from the fire hissed, crackled, and flew up into the air, where the wind scattered them across the sky. The sparks became beautiful golden stars, and they can still be seen high in the heavens today.

Rolla-Mano never did capture the girl who fled into the water. After a long search, he finally gave up and took the other girl to live with him forever in the sky. She is now the evening star. And from her spot in the heavens, she looks down upon the restless sea, the vast desert, and the kingdom of Rolla-Mano.

Desert Discovery

There are many symbols of the desert in dreamtime paintings. Circles are sometimes used to represent certain places, such as campsites or rock holes, or dreamtime events that have significance to the artist. Straight lines between circles usually represent the route traveled between camps. Small "u" shapes represent people sitting, and straight lines beside them usually represent their weapons. Most paintings are done in a variety of desert colors, mainly red, black, yellow, and white.

Make a Didgeridoo

This native instrument of Australia is said to be one of the oldest musical instruments in the world. In the aboriginal belief, the didgeridoo was an important part of their creation story, "sounding" the world into being in the dreamtime. Traditional didgeridoos are crafted from branches or tree trunks hollowed out by termites. They usually range in size from about 3 to 4 feet (.9 m to 1.2 m) in length. Some are much longer and even reach 8 feet (2.4 m)! Blowing into the end of the didgeridoo creates a one-of-a-kind sound. Years ago the instrument was played only by men during initiation ceremonies, but now you can make your own to try.

What You Need

- A grown-up to assist
- Masking tape
- 2 long wrapping paper tubes
- Paper cup
- Scissors
- Markers or paint

What You Do

1. Tape the two tubes together, end to end.
2. Place the paper cup over one end of the tube. Use tape to adhere it to the tube. Ask a grown-up to cut a slit in the bottom of the cup to form your mouthpiece.
3. Decorate your tube with markers or paint in the aboriginal art style. Look at pictures of didgeridoos on the Internet to give you some ideas for decorating your own.

4. To play your didgeridoo, sit in a chair and place the instrument in front of you, with the bottom resting on the floor. Place your mouth on the mouthpiece and make a low "motorboat" sound into the cup. Experiment with the sounds you can make. You might need to enlarge the hole in your mouthpiece to achieve the sound you want from your instrument.

Termite mound

Desert Discovery

Not all the formations in the outback are rock. Some of the most interesting ones are created by tiny termites. Termites eat leaf litter, grasses, soils, and wood, and there are more than 300 species of termites that construct nests. Some of the nests are underground, and others are very small, but the Spinifex termite creates the tall spires we see in the outback. These nests, called *Gun-boi* by the aborigines, can be over 20 feet (6 m) in height and can last as long as 50 years. Like a giant anthill, these nests are filled with a whole colony of insects, each with its own job. A queen termite rules the nest and can lay 500 eggs a day when she matures at five years of age. To keep the nest cool and comfortable in the hot desert, the termites build channels to provide ventilation through the mound. It's sort of like termite air-conditioning.

More About the Bindibu

Imagine yourself living in the outback like the Bindibu. This tribe knows how to make fire, but they do not use any drinking or cooking utensils. They lap up water at the water holes or from a clay pan, just as the animals that compete for the same water do.

Have you ever gone camping? What did you take with you to make it comfortable? Did you take a sleeping bag, equipment for cooking, a lantern, and drinking water? The Bindibu men travel to hunt without any of these comforts with them. While the men hunt, the women gather firewood and dig for roots to eat. Like all desert people, the Bindibu tribe must obtain water to survive. Sometimes they walk miles across the hot desert to find a small puddle to drink from. Try this Bindibu challenge to get a sense of what it would be like to be a Bindibu.

What You Need

- Bowl
- Water
- Stopwatch or watch with a second hand
- Paper
- Pen
- Glass of water

What You Do

1. Pour yourself a bowl full of water.

2. Wait until you are really thirsty. Now see if you can satisfy your thirst by using your tongue to lap up the water. Look at the watch and mark down the time, including seconds, that you begin drinking in this way. Drink.

3. When you've had enough water and no longer feel thirsty, stop, and look at the watch again. Mark down this end time.

4. Wait until you are thirsty again and then satisfy your thirst with a glass of water. Mark down your start and end time again. Which is a shorter period of time? Which satisfies your thirst more? Which is more fun? You can race your friends and see who can drink more water in less time!

So, how did you do with this challenge? Would you make a good Bindibu?

The Mountain Devil

There are many reptiles in the Australian deserts. In fact, there are about 600 species, including crocodiles, snakes, dragons, turtles, geckos, and tortoises. The mountain devil is just one of the many lizards that live in this desert. This scary-sounding creature is also known as the horned dragon and the thorny devil. Are you shaking in your boots? Don't be afraid. This is not a ferocious desert monster lurking in the Australian sands. It's a small, harmless, six-inch (15 cm) lizard. So what's all the fuss? Well, the *Moloch horridus*, or common mountain devil, is scary looking. It has many spines springing up from its head, back, arms, feet, and tail. These spines are actually just extensions of the scales found on many reptiles and are there to help defend it against predators. Ants are the mountain devil's food of choice. To battle the hot, dry desert, the mountain devil simply drinks the moisture that condenses on its skin each morning, just as many other desert reptiles do.

Mountain devil

Leapin' Lizards T-Shirt

Here's a great T-shirt to make to show the world you're wild about lizards.

What You Need

- A grown-up to assist
- Bubble wrap
- Scissors
- Fabric paint
- Paper plate
- Cardboard
- Clean, white T-shirt, washed without fabric softener

What You Do

1. Cut a lizard shape out of the sheet of bubble wrap.
2. Pour a thin layer of fabric paint onto the paper plate.

3. Dip the bubble wrap in fabric paint. Make sure that the paint is evenly spread on the bubbles on the bubble wrap. You don't want to get the areas in between full of paint.

4. Place the cardboard in the shirt so that the paint does not bleed through to the back.

5. Place the lizard shape down on the T-shirt, paint side down. Gently press the design onto the shirt, then gently lift off the bubble wrap. Fill your shirt with more lizards. Add different colors for a great look.

6. Let the shirt dry completely before wearing it.

Want to Be a Wallaby or a Wallaroo?

Wallabies and wallaroos, collectively considered kangaroos, are *macropods*, meaning "big foot." They are also *marsupials*, meaning they have pouches where their young develop and are fed. They can be found in the desert and other areas of Australia. Wallaroos are large kangaroos that are smaller than red or grey kangaroos, but larger than wallabies. They all eat grasses and shrubs. They are also extremely agile, as well as cute. Try this activity to see how you compare to a kangaroo.

What You Need

 Chalk

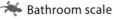 Bathroom scale

 Measuring tape

What You Do

1. Start by drawing a line outside on the ground with chalk. Stand on that line and see how far you and your friends can leap. Mark each spot you leap with chalk.

2. Compare that with a kangaroo's leaps. A red kangaroo can leap 39.3 feet (12 m). A Bennets wallaby can leap about 6.5 feet (2 m). Measure those distances with chalk to see how your leaps compare.

3. A red male kangaroo weighs about 143 to 187 pounds (65 to 85 kg). A Bennets wallaby weighs about 145 pounds (66 kg). Weigh yourself on the bathroom scale and see how your weight compares.

4. Last, compare your height to that of a red kangaroo, which is approximately 7.5 feet (2.3 m) tall. A Bennets wallaby is about 6.8 feet (2.1 m) tall. How tall are you?

Other Marsupials

Other marsupials besides the wallaby and the walla-roo call the outback home. There is the bilby, which is about the size of a rabbit and even hops like a rabbit. Unfortunately, this small marsupial with large ears and a long tail is endangered. The bilby lives underground in burrows to keep out of the heat of the desert. Its biggest predator is the European fox. The bilby has retreated deeper and deeper into the desert where the fox has not been able to follow. There are many species of Australian animals that did not survive after becoming endangered. The lesser bilby is one animal that became extinct in the 1930s. It was about a third of the size of the bilby still inhabiting the desert.

The numbat is another endangered Australian marsupial. It is chipmunk-sized and is the only Australian marsupial that feeds solely on ants and termites. It can eat about 20,000 insects a day.

Wallaby

On to the Arabian Desert

So, do you think you know why the deserts of Australia, known as the outback, are also called the "heart of Australia?" You'll have a bit of time to reflect on that question as we head to the Arabian Desert. Got your sunblock?

ARABIAN DAYS AND NIGHTS 7

The Arabian Desert covers about a million square miles (2,564,000 sq km) of the Arabian Peninsula. It is bordered by the Gulf of Suez on the east and by the Nile River on the west. About a third of the desert is covered with loose sand, a greater percentage than that of any other desert. Other areas of the desert are covered in gravel and rock. Unlike other deserts, it doesn't have any permanent rivers flowing across it or originating from it. The Arabian Desert sits between the Sahara and the Desert Corridor, a region that stretches from the Iranian Desert to the Gobi. Because of this location, the wildlife found in this desert comes from both Africa and Asia.

Some wildlife even comes from Europe, which is located to the north of the desert. Then there are some animals, such as the gazelle, that are believed to have developed in Arabia and spread to Africa and Asia. Let's begin our expedition to this extraordinary region.

Land of "a Thousand and One Nights"

You might have heard some of the tales from *A Thousand and One Nights*, written centuries ago. There are tales of Aladdin, Ali Baba and the forty thieves, Sinbad the sailor, and Scheherazade, to name a few. The story of Scheherazade features King Shahriyar, a distrustful man who did not trust his wives and had them killed. He vowed to have a new wife each night. Scheherazade invented a plan with her sister, Dunyzad. Scheherazade would tell her husband a story, but each night she would stop at a very crucial point. The king was anxious to hear the rest of the story and would let his wife live another day. The following night she would finish the story, but begin another, and so on. Eventually the king fell in love with her and stopped the killing. You'll find books in the Desert Resources section that contain this and other tales found in *A Thousand and One Nights*.

Desert Discovery

Look at the map to see all the countries in the Arabian Desert. You'll see that Kuwait, Saudi Arabia, Qatar, Yemen, the United Arab Emirates, and Oman are all located in the Arabian Desert. Parts of Iraq, Syria, and Jordan also lie in the desert.

Arabian Nights Party

What better way to get into the spirit of the Arabian Desert than to throw an Arabian Nights party for your friends? Here are some tips and activities for your party.

MAGIC CARPET INVITATIONS

What You Need

- A grown-up to assist
- Index cards
- Acrylic paint
- Paintbrush

- Gold glitter
- Scissors
- Pen or pencil

What You Do

1. Decorate your index cards with the acrylic paint to look like a magic carpet.

2. Sprinkle gold glitter on your design before your paint dries.

3. Cut a fringe on the two short sides of each card to look like the fringe on a carpet.

4. Write your invitation information on the back of your magic carpet.

5. Mail your magic carpet invitations in envelopes or pass them out to your friends.

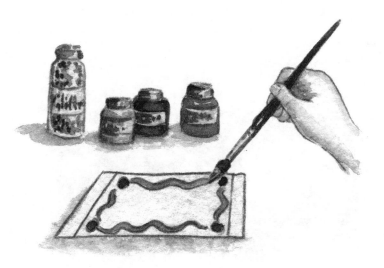

ARABIAN NIGHTS BUFFET

Set up a buffet for your party with some foods inspired by the Arabian Desert. You might want to include dates, olives, figs, pita bread, hummus, and tabouli (a salad of cracked wheat, tomatoes, parsley, mint, and more). Here's a quick recipe for a yummy hummus.

What You Need

- A grown-up to assist
- 2 15-ounce (425 g) cans chick peas, drained
- 1 tablespoon (15 ml) tahini
- 1 clove garlic
- Juice of one lemon
- Salt and pepper to taste
- Food processor or blender

- Spoon
- Plate
- Olive oil
- Pita bread
- Carrot sticks and other cut vegetables

4 servings

What You Do

1. Mix together the chick peas, tahini, garlic, lemon juice, salt, and pepper in the food processor or blender until the mixture is well-blended.

2. Spoon the hummus out onto a serving plate. Make a small indentation in the middle of the hummus with the back of the spoon and pour a little olive oil into the depression.

3. Serve with pita bread and cut veggies to dip in your hummus.

SULTAN'S TREASURE BOX

Traditional Egyptian jewelry boxes are inlaid with mother-of-pearl and are commonly decorated with geometric shapes. Between eating and games at your party, make treasure boxes for your guests to take home.

What You Need

- A grown-up to assist
- Newspapers
- Shoebox with lid, one per guest (or ask each guest to bring one)
- Gold spray paint
- Glue
- Jewel decorations

What You Do

1. Spread out newspapers on the ground in a well-ventilated area.

2. Spray each box and lid with the gold spray paint, following the canister's directions.

3. When the box and lid are completely dry, decorate them with the jewels and any other decorations you might want to add.

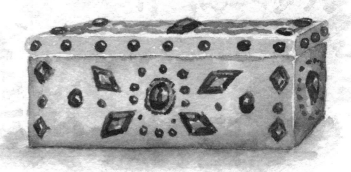

Quicksand and Quagmires

Can you imagine areas of *quicksand* and *quagmires* in the desert? You've probably seen actors in movies get swallowed up by quicksand, leading you to believe that quicksand is sort of like a living creature that can suck you down into a pit. Well, that's not how quicksand really works. The quicksand in the Arabian Desert is in an area known as the Rub al Khali, which is located in a region of the desert known as the Empty Quarter. It's an immense, sandy desert area, about the size of Texas, with little life. It's believed to be two million years old.

Quicksand is actually a mixture of sand and a grainy soil that is oversaturated with water, usually from an underground spring. What really happens is that the sand actually floats on the water. And it doesn't just occur in the Arabian Desert. Quicksand can form in many parts of the world with the right conditions.

So, what would you do if you really stepped into quicksand? You would begin to sink, but if you allowed your body to rest, you could actually float until someone came to help you out or you could paddle your way to safety.

Well, that tells us about quicksand, but there are also quagmires in the Arabian Desert. The quagmires of the desert are located along the Arabian coasts where there are salt flats called *sabkha*, a name that is derived from the Arabic term for "salt pan." These areas are very dangerous because their salty crust forms over soft mud.

Quicksand Experiment

Make your own quicksand with this easy experiment.

What You Need

- A grown-up to assist
- Hose
- Bucket with a small hole in the bottom to fit the nozzle of your hose
- Sand, enough to fill a bucket
- Rock
- Water

What You Do

1. Place the nozzle of the hose in the hole in the bottom of the bucket.
2. Fill the bucket with sand. Place a rock or some other object on the top of the sand.
3. Turn on the hose and allow water to slowly begin to fill the bucket. What happens to the rock as the bucket fills with water? At what point does the sand become quicksand? Shut the water off when the quicksand has formed. Put your hand in and feel the sand. How does it feel?

Oil Lies Underneath

You have probably heard the words *oil* and *Arabian Desert* together quite often. That is because oil, also called "liquid black gold," is one of the major resources in this region. Oil is found in many other places in the world, including under the ocean, in the polar regions, and in the rain forests. The oil in the desert is easy to remove because it is not covered with water, plants, or ice. Marco Polo witnessed oil collection in 1264 on his journey through Persia. In 1936 Standard Oil of California found oil under the sand in Saudi Arabia. Since that time the industry has grown dramatically. The Kingdom of Saudi Arabia has become one of the richest countries in the world.

In 1971 more than half the estimated world total of 450 billion barrels of oil came from desert areas. In 2002 the desert countries in this region produced about 25 percent of the world's oil.

How Much Oil Do You Use?

We are dependent on oil for many things. We use oil for gasoline, jet fuel, and diesel fuel. The petroleum oil that we import from the Arabian Desert is also used for heating fuels. Further refining of the petroleum oil creates petrochemicals that are used to make fertilizers, pesticides, sulfa drugs, and even women's stockings, which are made from nylon. Do you have plastic in your house? Well, plastic is another substance that is created from petroleum. How about things made from polyester (a stretchable fabric used in clothing) or polyethylene (a protective coating used on hardwood floors and wood furniture)? How much oil do you use at your house? Let's find out.

What You Need

 Pad

 Pencil

What You Do

1. Start by making a list of all the things you can think of that use oil in your house and write them down. Write down how many cars you have. If you use oil to heat or cook with, write that down also.

2. After your preliminary list is completed, go on a scavenger hunt around your house for things made from oil. How many objects can you find that are made from plastic? Polyester? Polyethylene?

3. Ask your parent if anyone in your house has ever had a sulfa antibiotic, such as Bactrim, when they were sick. If anyone has, add that to the list. How long is your list already?

4. Sit down with your family when you have completed your list and see if there are any ways that you can cut down on your use of oil or oil products. Show them your list.

Arabian oryx

Wildlife Then and Now

More than 100,000 years ago the Arabian Desert was a lush, green area where elephants, lions, and rhinos roamed. Climate changes altered the environment. The lush, green areas became a desert and the elephants, lions, and rhinos became extinct.

Now there is a wildlife preserve that is trying to prevent desert wildlife from suffering a similar fate. Arabia's Wildlife Center in the United Arab Emirates is the home to the largest collection of the Arabian Peninsula's wildlife. There are more than 1,200 critters at the center, including many that are endangered. There are snakes, foxes, gazelles, rodents, lizards, and baboons. There are also some very rare animals, like the Arabian leopard, the Rock Hyrax, and the Arabian Oryx. Through education the organization hopes to raise awareness about the great diversity that is found among desert wildlife. The center attracts more than 100,000 people each year.

The Nomadic Hedgehog

The hedgehog might not come to your mind as a desert mammal, but in fact the hedgehogs of the Arabian Peninsula have been around for about 20 million years, with few changes. Three species live in this region, and they all are well adapted to the harsh desert climate. Like most desert animals, hedgehogs leave their resting spots at sunset and hunt for insects, lizards, and snakes to eat throughout the cool night.

Hedgehogs are well protected from many predators by the spines on their bodies. They are tough little creatures, and they put up quite a fight against desert snakes. Though they are small, they can withstand numerous stings from bees and other insects.

The hedgehog population has withstood the human encroachment that has caused many other animal populations to dwindle. This may be because hedgehogs are extremely resistant to the scarcity of food and water. In a laboratory setting they can sometimes go weeks without food or water.

Play the Hedgehog Web Game

Hedgehogs are just one part of the desert food web in the Arabian Peninsula. Play this game with your friends to see what part hedgehogs play in this giant web.

What You Need

 10 to 15 friends

 Ball of yarn

What You Do

1. Assign each of your friends a part in the food web. Assign lizards, insects, snakes, hedgehogs, and owls. Have everyone stand in a circle.

2. Begin by holding the ball of yarn in your hand. Hold onto the string and toss the ball to an insect. That insect should throw the ball to another insect while still holding the string.

3. Continue playing by tossing the yarn ball to all the insects. Then ask the players which creatures eat the insects, and begin tossing the yarn ball to them. Keep tossing the ball of yarn until all the creatures have eaten another creature on the food web. The owls should be the last creatures to toss the yarn ball.

4. Everyone should be holding the string, and a web should be formed in the inside of the circle.

5. Now ask all the creatures to let go of their string if pesticides would harm them. The insects would be killed first because the pesticides are designed to kill them. What happens to the animals that normally eat the insects? What happens to the web? You can see that the loss of just a small part of the web may mean the loss of many other parts of the web. What are some other things that humans do that might harm the desert creatures? Is there a market for fur for any of these animals? What about food? Which creatures are affected? What happens to the web?

The Bedouins, People of the Desert

The word *Bedouin* comes from the Arabic word *bedu*, meaning "inhabitant of the desert." There are actually two groups of people known as the Bedouins— the Negev and the Sinai. Both are nomadic, and for thousands of years, they traveled from desert oasis to desert oasis by camel in search of water and food. Today many of these people live a less nomadic life; however, there are many who still follow the traditional ways of their ancestors.

Both the men and the women of this culture wear flowing robes, just as some other desert people do. It is customary for the Bedouins to live in tents that have two rooms separated by a woven curtain. One side of the tent is called the *mag'ad*, or sitting place, and is reserved for men only. The other side, called *maharama*, or place of the women, is just that, a place for women to entertain guests and prepare meals.

Bedouin meals are made with ingredients easily obtained in the desert. For example, like the people of the Sahara, the Bedouins rely on dates as a staple ingredient. Their meals are also made with rice, yogurt

made from goat's milk, goat or camel meat, the milk from these animals, and wild berries that are found in the region.

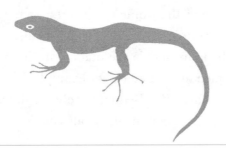

Time to Leave

After you've enjoyed some Bedouin hospitality, it's time to be on our way to a desert where a cup of tea would feel mighty nice. We're heading to a much colder climate, but a desert nonetheless! So be prepared for some cooler days and nights ahead.

NOT ALL DESERTS ARE HOT 8

Wow, we've seen cold deserts, but nothing *this* cold. Who would believe that the Arctic, with all that snow, actually has a desert? Let's go back to the physical definition of a desert. Deserts have less than 19.7 inches (50 cm) of rain each year. The areas we are now going to explore, Antarctica and Greenland, range in annual precipitation from 5.9 to 10.2 inches (15 to 26 cm), well under the desert requirements. Even during winters of heavy snowfall, the annual precipitation still falls under the 19.7-inch (50-cm) guideline.

Do you remember any of the temperatures we have experienced in other deserts? Most were pretty hot. Well, we know these deserts are not hot. Arctic temperatures range from −40°F (−40°C) to 70°F (21°C) and Antarctic temperatures range from −70°F (−57°C) to 32°F (0°C). Is that as cold as you thought it would be? Let's go exploring.

Starting at the Bottom

For some, Antarctica is considered the bottom of the world. It is the most southern point on our planet. Look for the continent on a globe or a map. We're going to explore the McMurdo Dry Valleys, a cold desert that covers 1,853 square miles (4,800 sq km) of southeastern Antarctica. It is one of the most intriguing areas on our planet for scientists to study because, on a continent of ice, these areas are bare.

Antarctica was not always a frozen sheet of ice. Through the discovery of fossils we know that it was once populated with dinosaurs and was quite possibly a temperate rainforest. It is believed that during this period there were only a few Alpine glaciers and some small ice caps. How did it become the icy continent it is today? That is up for debate. Scientists believe that the formation of Antarctica as an icy continent took

place over a period of 50,000 years. Why it happened is a question that divides scientists. Until recently, most scientists followed a theory known as *thermal isolation*. This theory deals with the movement of the large supercontinent, called *Pangaea* (pan-JE-a), that existed at that time. It's believed that Antarctica formed when Pangaea broke apart and other landmasses shifted in the oceans. Another group of scientists recently came out with another theory. They believe that the movement of the landmasses did have an effect, but they believe that there were other factors as well, including the movement of heat in the oceans, carbon dioxide levels in the atmosphere, and the movement of the earth. Both are theories that will continue to be studied for a long time.

Scientists study many things about Antarctica. They flock to Antarctica to study primitive life forms, such as blue-green algae and freeze-dried microscopic worms, and to see this area where time has stood still for millions of years.

The Taylor Valley, discovered in the McMurdo Dry Valleys in 1903 by explorer Robert F. Scott, is called the "valley of the dead" because there is so little life there. Scott reported that his party did not see anything living—not even moss—when he first explored the region. Scott did not have the tools to really explore the life in this valley in 1903, but scientists do have them now. Scientists have found that it is not as dead or lifeless as

Scott believed. Under the soils and frozen lakes is an entire ecosystem of algal mats, phytoplankton (plant plankton), and worms. These organisms are helping scientists to study the history of life on our planet. They might also be able to give scientists clues to life on other planets, such as Mars.

Plankton Net

You don't have to go to Antarctica to look at plankton. *Plankton* are very tiny organisms that float around in all bodies of water. You can find them in a local pond or in the ocean. The tricky thing is that plankton are so small that you can't see them just by looking at the water. You will need to make a net, catch them, and look at them under a microscope. Here's how to make your own net to catch plankton.

What You Need
- A grown-up to assist
- 5 pipe cleaners (chenille stem)
- 1 knee-high nylon stocking
- Duct tape
- Scissors
- 1 8-ounce (240-ml) plastic bottle of water
- String
- Eyedropper
- Glass slide
- Microscope

Phytoplankton

What You Do

1. Create a circle using two of the pipe cleaners. Attach the other three pipe cleaners evenly around the circle. Twist the ends together to connect the three pipe cleaners.

2. Wrap the open end of the stocking around the circle. Hold it in place with the duct tape.

3. Cut off the foot of the stocking.

4. Place the bottle opening at the ankle end of the stocking. Wrap the stocking around the bottle and secure it with duct tape. The plankton will collect in the bottle while you are using the net.

5. Tie a string to the pipe cleaners to pull the net along in the pond or ocean water. Use your net by dragging it along in the water while you're wading.

6. Now it's time to look at the plankton you caught with your net. Use the dropper to collect a few drops of water from the bottle.

7. Squeeze a couple of the drops onto a glass slide and place it under the microscope. Do you see the tiny plankton moving about on your slide? How many different kinds can you find? Draw a picture of one and see if you can identify it using a plankton guidebook.

Why Are the Dry Valleys Dry?

We've seen why other deserts are dry; now let's look at why these cold deserts are so dry in this land of ice and snow. Like other deserts, dry winds blowing across this region carry little humidity and don't create much precipitation. Mountains block humid winds that blow from the Ross Sea.

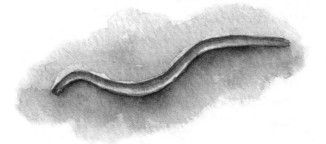

Desert Discovery

The tiny nematode worms in the Antarctic desert are not your everyday, garden-variety earthworm. These are microscopic worms that are not segmented, meaning that their bodies are smooth and often tapered at both ends. They are about .04 of an inch (.1 cm) long. That's smaller than a grain of rice. Now that's small!

If you dug into the soil at your house, you would probably find a bunch of earthworms in it. This is not the case in the Antarctic Desert. You could dig out a sample of soil in this region and not find a single worm as we know them. Nematodes may be hard to find, but in this desert these worms are the top of the food chain, feeding on bacteria and other microscopic organisms. Some scientists refer to the nematodes as the "lions of the Dry Valleys" and even call themselves "worm herders."

Heading to the Far North

It's time to head from the most southern point in the world to the most northern point in the world. Flying to the far north arctic region of the world, we find the country of Greenland. Greenland is the largest non-continental island in the world, and 84 percent of its area is ice-capped. In this land of the midnight sun lies the desert of Ultima Thule (UL-teema TOO-lee), named by explorer Captain Cook on his expedition to the region in 1778. This desert area in the district of Avanersuaq can be found in the north of Greenland about 990 miles (1600 km) from the capital, Nuuk.

Northern Lights Skyscape

There are some natural phenomena due to the position of Greenland and the clarity of the Arctic air. Sometimes the sunlight causes the sea and the sky to appear as one. This can cause people to feel upside-down when they are paddling a kayak in the water. Another phenomenon is the Fata Morgana, which is a mirage effect caused by reflections off the water that causes people to see solid objects that don't really exist, such as ships, forests, and even cities. The other phe-nomenon is the northern lights, or aurora borealis, which is caused by particles from the sun that get trapped in the earth's magnetic field. The sky swirls, shimmers, and pulses with multicolored light. You might have even seen the waves of color in the night sky where you live. The farther north you live, the greater chance you have to see them.

Many artists have tried to capture the beauty of the northern lights in their work. Here's your chance to use the northern lights as your own inspiration.

What You Need
- Watercolor paper or matte board
- Oil pastels including white, yellow, light green, and black
- Paintbrush
- Water
- Watercolor paints including deep blue, purple, and black
- Coarse salt (optional)

What You Do

1. Draw the northern lights on your paper with the lighter colored oil pastels. Keep in mind that the northern lights appear like waves of color in the sky. Don't fill up the entire paper with the pastels because you will need to leave room for sky.

2. Use the black oil pastel to draw some outlines of trees on the bottom of your page. These will appear as silhouettes in your finished picture.

3. Paint the entire page with water. Add your watercolor sky colors to the entire page. Remember, a night sky is not black. It's made up of deep blues and purples. Experiment with your colors to achieve the perfect sky. The watercolors will not stick to the oil pastels. Your northern lights will shine through your finished picture.

4. For an extra pop, sprinkle a tiny bit of coarse salt in the sky while the paint is still wet. Brush the salt off when the picture is completely dry. Have fun and be creative!

Tundra

Tundra is another term used for the polar desert. There are two kinds of tundra—the *arctic tundra*, which is the northernmost limit of plant growth that circles the north pole, and the *alpine tundra*, which is found at high mountain elevations. There is little *biodiversity* in the tundra, meaning that there is not a great variety of wildlife species here, as there is in the rain forest. The thin layer of soil that covers the ground is known as *permafrost*. It is always frozen. In the summer the very top of the permafrost layer may thaw for a short time, enabling plants and microorganisms to continue their cycle.

Knud Rasmussen, Arctic Explorer

To many people, Robert Peary is the most famous explorer of this region. Certainly we know that Captain Cook also explored the region, but Greenlanders consider Knud Rasmussen to be the first explorer here. While other explorers were coming to the region to search for an alternate route to China for trade purposes, Knud Rasmussen was a native Greenlander, born to native Inuit and Danish parents in 1879. Growing up in Greenland, he learned to kayak and ride a dogsled.

He loved the Arctic and grew up to explore the region, studying the wildlife, people, and climate. He became the first person to travel the Northwest Passage by dogsled. Between 1912 and 1919 he made several expeditions, but his most famous "Great Sledge Journey" to collect Inuit songs and legends began in 1921 and was completed in 1924. During that journey he traveled 29,000 miles (46,700 km) across the Arctic.

Most of what is known about the region is due to the work of Rasmussen and his books.

Ultima Thule Wildlife

This cold desert is not as barren as the one in Antarctica. Greenland has birch trees that grow to about 20 feet (6 m) high, and in late summer areas are carpeted with wildflowers, including Arctic poppies, dandelion, and berries. These plants are able to support a variety of Greenland wildlife, including caribou, lemmings, and musk ox. Polar bears and Arctic foxes also wander onto the frozen ice pack. The icy waters off the coast also support whales, walruses, and seals.

Desert Discovery

We've seen sand dunes in many of the deserts we have visited. Of course, there are no sand dunes in the polar deserts, but there are snow dunes. In areas that get more precipitation in the form of snow, dunes do form in these polar deserts.

The Great White Bear, Tornassuk

Tornassuk, meaning "the master of helping spirits," is the name Greenlanders use for the polar bear. Polar bears are the "lions of the Arctic," feeding on whales, seals, and anything else they can get their paws on. This is certainly quite a difference from the tiny nematode in the Dry Valleys, isn't it? Polar bears move across the ice and water from Alaska all the way to Russia by way of Canada, Greenland, and northern Norway. The International Agreement for the Conservation of Polar Bears, created in 1973, set out to protect the polar bear populations in these countries. Since then, the Norwegian population of polar bears has nearly doubled in size. Even so, native people in Greenland and the other arctic regions have the right to continue their tradition of hunting the bears for food and fur. They kill more than 700 bears each year.

Feel the Heat

Polar bears are so well insulated by a thick layer of blubber, which can be more than four inches (10.2 cm) thick, that they give off no heat. This helps the polar bear survive in the extreme temperatures of Greenland, but it also means that polar bears can overheat when running and expending a lot of energy. Do you want to know what that extra layer of blubber feels like? Try this simple experiment to find out.

What You Need

- 2 resealable plastic sandwich bags
- Shortening
- Bowl of ice water

What You Do

1. Fill one sandwich bag with shortening.

2. Turn the other bag inside out and place it in the bag with the shortening. Securely seal the two bags together to form a blubber sleeve for you to slip your hand into.

3. Place one hand in the blubber sleeve, then submerge both hands into the bowl of ice water. Which hand gets colder quicker? Describe the difference the blubber makes.

People of the Desert

Roughly 650 people inhabit the Avanersuaq, or Qaanaaq, region, the only municipality in North Greenland. Most are of Inuit ancestry. Others are descended from Norsemen from Norway and Denmark when those two countries controlled Greenland. Greenland finally won the right from Denmark to govern itself in 1979, but was still under Denmark's control. It gained complete independence in 1998.

The people of Greenland speak Greenlandic, which is related to Inupiak, the language spoken by the Inuit people. While Greenlandic is the official language, Danish and English are also spoken. The Greenlandic language underwent a spelling change in 1973. The long vowel letters *a, e, i, o, u*, were replaced with *aa, ee, ii, oo, uu*, and the letter *k* was replaced with *q*. It is difficult to find pronunciation keys to many Greenlandic words, but you might try to say the word *Qaanaaq* as "kay nayk."

The people here eat a lot of fish, whale meat, and reindeer, just like other Arctic people. Unlike the people in the hot deserts, these people need to dress warmly to protect themselves from the harsh climate. Sometimes it is warm enough to go outside in a T-shirt, but strangely enough the next day there could be a blizzard. Like other desert people, those in Greenland are adapted to a very harsh climate.

Where to Next?

Well, our journey is over. We have seen deserts full of
sand and others covered in ice. We have explored salt
flats and canyons, dunes and burrows. Where to next?
Well, it's time to head home and see what issues face
some of these deserts and what we can do to help.

SAVING THE SANDS 9

There are many issues facing deserts around our world. In some regions we have seen deserts expanding, while in others we have seen deserts shrinking. In some areas we have seen desert wildlife become endangered or extinct. Now it's time to confront some of these issues and find out what is being done or what can be done to help protect these ecosystems in the future. If you live in a desert area, there are many things that you can do to make a difference in your own area, but even if you don't live near a desert there are things that you can do to help.

Hold Back the Desert

We have already seen how people can cause areas surrounding deserts to experience desertification. Some deserts grow and shrink naturally. This natural process is called *desertization*. The region of Sahel in northern Africa experienced the growth of the desert through both of these processes. First, the area experienced a lot of rain during the 1960s, which made grass grow. The greenery attracted nomads, who dug wells and herded cattle. This caused desertification.

Then there was a 20-year period when there was no rainfall. This caused a drought that increased the desert's size. Cattle trampled the ground around the wells. They also ate all the plants. All of this caused more desertification. The nomads had also planted a lot of crops to sell during the rainy period. The crops used up all of the nutrients in the land—more desertification. The land was eventually turned into a wasteland and many people died.

So what could have been done to prevent desertification? Since rainfall can't be controlled, people have to look at what they can do to hold back the sands of the deserts. Here are some ways people can help hold back the sands.

1. Plant trees and protect trees that surround desert areas. The trees help prevent erosion by holding the soil in place and keeping the topsoil, with its vital nutrients, from blowing away. For example, the people of Ethiopia are planting trees that don't require much water. The United Nations has even distributed small stoves to people in some of these regions. The stoves require less wood than that needed when cooking over an open fire.

2. Farmers can raise smaller herds so that there won't be the problem of overgrazing. When there are fewer animals eating the grass, more grass continues to grow and hold the soil.

3. Another way that farmers can help is to stop plowing their fields in straight lines. If they use *contour* plowing, plowing in curves, the wind does not blow as much topsoil away.

Xeriscape!

Have you seen sprinklers on for hours, trying to irrigate or water gardens in your area? A sprinkler can spray about 300 gallons of water each hour. This can be a tremendous waste of a precious resource in desert communities and other areas.

In the early 1980s Denver Water set out to provide a creative landscaping plan to help conserve water in

Colorado's arid regions. The plan is called Xeriscape (ZERA-scape). Nancy Leavitt, a Denver Water environmental planner, created the word from the Greek word *xeros*, meaning "dry" and *scape*, from the word *landscape*. Xeriscape is, therefore, a plan for landscaping in dry, desert areas. Its focus is to conserve water.

Other areas are now using the seven principles of this plan to conserve water in their regions. In fact, xeriscape programs now exist in more than 40 states.

It is important to conserve water everywhere, not just in desert communities, so encourage your friends and family to use these principles to conserve water on their properties. You can also help by writing letters to government officials in desert areas to use xeriscape methods of landscaping on public lands.

Here are some xeriscape tips to follow for your own landscape project that you and an adult can share:

1. Have a plan. Planning is the first step in every project. Think about how you want to design your landscape. It helps if you first make a sketch of the area. Work with an adult to estimate how much this project will cost and what maintenance it will need to keep it looking nice. You should also think about the help you might need to complete your project.

2. Test your soil. If you can, bring a sample of your soil to your local cooperative extension office for testing. They will be able to tell you the composition of your soil and if you need to add anything to your soil, such as fertilizers or lime, before you begin planting.

3. Select appropriate plants. This can be a lot of fun. This is also where the "dry" gardening plan comes into play. You should select plants for your landscape that don't require much watering. Here's your chance to explore your local garden center for the right plants that will conserve water in your garden. Look for native plants that have adapted to local dry desert conditions. You will be able to combine some of these local varieties with some more exotic varieties that also require less water. Ask the specialists in your garden center for some help selecting these plants for your region. Explain your project to them.

4. Maintain. Your garden should require less work to maintain than other gardens that require more water. Ask your garden center how to take care of your plantings.

5. Mulch. Use mulch in areas to keep moisture around your plants and to lessen the effects of evaporation. Your garden center specialists can help you pick out the right mulch for your garden.

Desert Plants for Sale

So, you have planned a garden in your area and you have decided to plant some local desert plants to follow the principles we just discussed. Instead of heading to the local garden center, you decide to head off to the desert near your home and dig up a few for your garden. Good idea? No!

Believe it or not, some people think that this is a good idea, and some even sell these dug-up plants to unsuspecting people looking for a cactus for their garden. Removing plants from the wild contributes to desertification. In addition, many plants that are removed from their natural areas do not survive the transplanting process. Be sure to purchase desert plants from a good nursery or garden center to ensure that they have not been taken out of the wild.

Horned lizard

Where Are the Lizards?

Many populations of desert wildlife have seen a serious decline in their numbers because of a number of factors. The capture of wild lizards and other desert wildlife for the pet trade is one reason for this decline. Some are suffering from the loss of habitat. More houses and people in the desert regions equal less room for wildlife. Desert animals are also in trouble because of the introduction of alien, or nonnative, species of animals in their habitats. These nonnative animals sometimes eat the same food as the native animals, causing shortages.

Horned lizards, or horny toads, as they are called, have experienced a decline in their population because of all of these reasons. There are 13 species of horned lizards in North America. Amazing to watch, these lizards can actually inflate their bodies to look like little spiny balloons for protection. One species of horned lizard, the Texas horned lizard, has already disappeared in east and central Texas, and is decreasing in numbers in the north. Other species in the Southwest are also in trouble.

Aside from overcollection for the pet trade and loss of habitat, horned lizards are dealing with an exotic ant that has been introduced to their habitat. Horned lizards eat ants, but not these ants. Unfortunately, these ants compete for the same habitat as the ants the lizards do eat. If these exotic, or alien, ants overtake the habitat, then the horned lizards lose a source of food.

The horned lizards are not the only desert creatures with declining populations. Many desert species face similar problems. You can help by not buying pets that may have been taken from wild desert areas. Ask at pet stores for lizards and snakes that have been bred in captivity.

You can also help by supporting land management so that these crucial habitats are not lost.

Pygmy owl

Urban Sprawl Wipes Out Habitat

You have seen that many desert species have declined because they have lost vital desert habitat. Let's take a closer look at this loss of habitat and why it occurs. There are many areas in the American Southwest and other desert areas around the world that suffer from urban sprawl. *Urban sprawl* occurs when cities spread out into the areas surrounding them because of all the people moving there. This is occurring at dangerous rates in Pima County, Arizona, as well as in areas of San Diego County, the Bellona Wetlands in Los Angeles, and the San Joaquin Valley in California.

The development of these areas has been poorly planned and a bit out of control. It not only creates a loss of habitat for desert wildlife, but it also creates additional pollution. According to the Center for Biological Diversity, the population of Tucson, Arizona, and surrounding Pima County has exploded in recent years. The population grew by 200,000 people over the 10-year period between 1990 and 2000.

Conservationists at the center and other environmental groups have been working to monitor species in this region. They have used the Endangered Species Act to help save some crucial habitat for endangered species in this region, including the pygmy owl.

Here are ways that you can help:

1. Read the newspaper with your parents or watch the local news to keep informed about development and issues that affect crucial desert habitats.

2. If you are concerned about development in your area, write to the local planning board or other community officials about your concerns.

3. Participate in local nature preserve clean-up days and other events that are sponsored by groups working to preserve desert habitats. Show your support!

4. Join the ecology club at your school or speak to your teacher about starting one. This is a great way to get information out to your classmates and friends.

Purposeful Postcards

Here's a way to make your own postcards to announce a club meeting or a desert event, or to voice your concerns to a local official.

What You Need
- Ruler
- Cardstock (6 inches × 4½ inches, 15.24 cm × 11.43 cm)
- Black marker
- Green ink pad
- Markers (optional)

What You Do

1. Place the ruler in the middle of the card and draw a black line. That will divide your writing space on the left from your address space on the right.

2. Flip the card over and begin your design. To create a cactus, place your thumb on the stamp pad and then press the ink onto the postcard. Create the spines on your cactus using the black marker.

3. Experiment with your design. You might want to draw other desert pictures on your card with your other markers. Be creative and show your support of desert preservation!

Use Less Oil

We have seen that tremendous numbers of oil wells have been drilled in the Arabian Desert for extraction and exploration. These are a strain on the desert environment. Greater strains on the desert are oil wells that catch fire and burn for months, as well as oil spills on the desert sands. This region has been in political turmoil for many, many years and the desert ecosystem has not been a priority during this time. Because of this, the desert ecosystem has suffered. Although it may seem like we can't lessen the turmoil and stress in this region, we can do things at home to help lessen our dependency on the oil of this region and other desert regions.

Here's how you can help:

1. It takes energy to make the packaging we use. Packaging includes plastic wrap, paper, and plastic containers. Think about what you buy when you go shopping with your parents. Shop for items that use less packaging.

2. Cars burn fuel from the desert and other vital habitats in our world, such as the oceans and rain forests. Encourage your parents to buy cars that are fuel-efficient. Use public transportation, bicycles, or walk instead of driving whenever possible to do so safely.

3. Buy less plastic. Substitute glass containers that are reusable for disposable plastic containers. Purchase clothing made from natural fabrics instead of synthetic fabrics. Use reusable containers to store your leftovers.

4. Ask your parents to purchase energy-efficient appliances for your home that will use less energy. They will end up saving money and helping the environment.

Make a Difference

There are always going to be new challenges and issues facing the deserts of our world. Fortunately, we have some of the most spectacular deserts right here in the United States, making it much easier to get involved in desert preservation. Check out the Desert Resources section for organizations that are working to conserve deserts throughout the world, such as Desert Watch, based in Tucson, Arizona. You can find their Web site and many others in the following pages. Check out the Web sites for more information and keep yourself informed about these fascinating places on our planet. You can work to make a difference wherever you live. Your efforts to protect all our crucial ecosystems will be long lasting.

DESERT RESOURCES

Favorite Books, Videos, and Web Sites

░░

CHAPTER 1: DISCOVERING DESERTS

Books

Anderson, Edward. *The Cactus Family*. Portland, OR: Timber Press, 2001.

Hazen-Hammond, Susan. *The Great Saguaro Book*. Berkeley, CA: Ten Speed Press, 1997.

Simon, Seymour. *Deserts*. New York: William Morrow & Co., 1990.

Web Sites

Learn more about the Rainbow Bridge National Monument at www.lapahie.com/Rainbow_Natural_Bridge.cfm

More information about grafting cacti is available at www.cacti.co.il/grafting.htm

CHAPTER 2: WELCOME TO THE WILD WEST

Books

Benjamin, Cynthia. *Footprints in the Sand*. New York: Cartwheel Books, 1999.

Brett, Jan. *Armadillo Rodeo*. New York: Penguin Putnam, 1995.

Goodman, Susan E. *Ultimate Field Trip 2: Digging into Southwest Archeology*. New York: Aladdin Paperbacks, 2000.

Guiberson, Brenda. *Cactus Hotel*. Madison, WI: Turtleback Books, 1993.

Thompson, Ida. *National Audubon Society Field Guide to North American Fossils*. New York: Alfred A. Knopf, 1982.

Web Sites

For more information about the American Forests National Register of Big Trees, visit www.americanforests.org.

For information on desert travel, creatures, and plants, check out www.desertusa.com.

Learn more about the Navajo in the Southwest at www.americanwest.com/pages/navajo2.htm.

Learn more about the Sonoran Desert Exhibit at www.nczoo.org.

Plan a visit or take an online tour of the Arizona Sonora Desert Museum at www.desertmuseum.org/index.html.

Check out these Web sites for prickly pear recipes: www.totacc.com/user/jgoucher/pprecipe.htm and www.gourmetsleuth.com/nopalitos_list.htm.

Try the prickly pear ice recipe at www.melborponsti.com/first/first015.shtml.

Learn more about the Sonoran Desert at the Arizona-Sonora Desert Museum's Web site: www.desertmuseum.org.

To find out more about the Petrified Forest National Park, check out www.petrified.forest.national-park.com.

Visit the Petroglyph National Monuments Web site at www.nps.gov/petr.

You can find dinosaur excavation kits for kids at www.twoguysfossils.com.

CHAPTER 3: SOUTH OF THE BORDER

Books

Chatwin, Bruce and Paul Theroux. *Nowhere Is a Place: Travels in Patagonia*. San Francisco, CA: Sierra Club Books, 1985.

Web Sites

Learn more about flamingos, hear their call, and find out about flamingo adoptions at www.geocities.com/RainForest/Jungle/7751/fmgo.html.

Check out a map of Patagonia at www.orient.k12.wa.us/patagoniadesert.htm.

Explore Argentina at the Argentina for Tourists Web site: www.austral.addr.com/patagonia/photo.htm.

CHAPTER 4: JOURNEY TO THE SAHARA, NAMIB, KALAHARI, AND NEGEV

Books

Owens, Mark and Delia. *Cry of the Kalahari*. Boston, MA: Houghton Mifflin, 1984.

Reynolds, Jan. *Sahara*. New York: Harcourt Brace Jovanovich, 1991.

Swift, Jeremy. *The Sahara (The World's Wild Places)*. Amsterdam, The Netherlands: Time Life Books, 1975.

Web Sites

Look at the pictures of desert animals at the Enchanted Learning site at www.enchantedlearning.com/biomes/desert/desert.shtml.

Check out some dunes in the United States deserts at www.desertusa.com/magjan98/dunes/jan_dune1.html.

See your name translated into Egyptian Hieroglyphs at www.guardians.net/egypt/hieroglyphs/hiero-translator.htm.

Take a Namib trivia quiz at the Living Edens site at www.pbs.org/edens/namib/trivia.htm.

See the fennec fox and other animals of the San Antonio Zoo at www.sazoo.org.

Video

Etosha: Africa's Untamed Wilderness. The Living Edens/Reader's Digest, ABC/Kane Productions International, 1997.

CHAPTER 5: THE RED AND BLACK DESERTS OF ASIA

Books

Facklam, Margery. *Tracking Dinosaurs in the Gobi*. New York: Twenty-First Century Books, 1998.

Web Sites

Learn more about the wildlife of the Gobi Desert at www.oneearthadventures.com/gobi/wildlife/wildlife.htm.

Learn more about snow leopards at www.snowleopard.org.

Explore the Gobi Desert of Mongolia at http://baatar.freeyellow.com.

CHAPTER 6: DESERTS DOWN UNDER

Books

Fox, Mem. *Possum Magic*. New York: Gulliver Books, 1990.

Germein, Katrina. *Big Rain Coming*. New York: Houghton Mifflin, 2000.

Morin, Paul. *Animal Dreaming: An Aboriginal Dreamtime Story*. New York: Silver Whistle Press, 1998.

Web Sites

Find links to Australian dreamtime stories at www.aboriginalartwork.com/culture.html.

Look at Aboriginal Dreamings Web site for dreamtime paintings and their meanings at www.ozebiz.com.au/dreamings/meaning.html.

See Australian animals at www.australianexplorer.com.

Learn more about Australian conservation at the Australian Conservation Foundation's site at www.acfonline.org.au/asp/pages/home.asp.

CHAPTER 7: ARABIAN DAYS AND NIGHTS

Books

Ben-Ezer, Ehud. *Hosni the Dreamer: An Arabian Tale*. New York: Farrar Strauss Giroux, 1997.

Kimmel, Eric A. *The Tale of Aladdin and the Wonderful Lamp: A Story from the Arabian Nights*. New York: Holiday House, 1992.

Web Sites

Learn more about the history of petroleum at www.classroomenergy.org/teachers/petroleum/aboutpetroleum02.html.

CHAPTER 8: NOT ALL DESERTS ARE HOT

Books

Woodford, Chris. *Arctic Tundra and Polar Deserts*. Austin, TX: Raintree/Steck Vaughn, 2002.

Web Sites

See paintings inspired by the northern lights at www.streetmorrisart.com/northernlightsartgalleryl.html.

Print out and color a Greenlander mask at www.enchantedlearning.com/artists/greenland/coloring/mask1.shtml.

Look at pictures of Ultima Thule at http://ultimathulelodge.com/wildlife/wildlife1.htm.

Learn more about polar bears at www.polarbearsalive.org.

CHAPTER 9: SAVING THE SANDS

Web Sites

To find your local Cooperative Extension Service, look up your local 4-H group or go to the national Web site at www.fourhcouncil.edu.

Organizations

There are many organizations working to conserve deserts around the world. Here are some to take a look at and support.

Coalition for Sonoran Desert Protection
300 E. University, #120
Tucson, AZ 85705
(520) 388-9925
www.sonorandesert.org
Over 40 conservation and community groups formed the Coalition for Sonoran Desert Protection in 1998 after the pygmy owl was placed on the Endangered Species List. Today the coalition is working to establish the strongest species and habitat protections possible under the Sonoran Desert Conservation Plan (SDCP).

Desert Watch
4420 West Cortaro Farms Road
Tucson, AZ 85742
(520) 744-0931
www.desertwatch.org
Desert Watch is an independent, nonprofit organization based in Tucson, Arizona. It is a partnership between scientists, private landowners, indigenous peoples, grassroots and national conservation organizations, resource managers,

and government agencies dedicated to developing an arid lands conservation strategy for North America.

National Wildlife Federation

11100 Wildlife Center Drive

Reston, VA 20190

(800) 822-9919

www.nwf.org

The National Wildlife Federation is a large, member-supported conservation group designed to educate, inspire, and assist individuals and organizations of diverse cultures to protect the environment and preserve wildlife.

The Nature Conservancy

4245 North Fairfax Drive, Suite 100

Arlington, VA 22203

(703) 841-5300

http://nature.org

The Nature Conservancy's mission is to preserve the plants, animals, and natural communities that represent the diversity of life on earth by protecting the lands and waters they need to survive. They have already protected over 116 million acres in North America, South America, Asia, the Caribbean, Central America, and other areas.

Places to Visit

There are many places to visit in the United States to experience desert ecosystems. Many zoos in the country have desert ecosystem exhibits that are worth visiting. Check out the one nearest you.

Here are some additional places in America's desert states that you will love.

ARIZONA

Arizona-Sonora Desert Museum

2021 N. Kinney Road

Tucson, AZ 85743

http://desertmuseum.org/index.html

Canyon de Chelly National Monument

Box 588

Chinle, AZ 86503

(520) 674-5500

www.americansouthwest.net/arizona/canyon_de_chelly/national_monument.html

Chiricahua National Monument
Dos Cabezas Route Box 6500
Willcox, AZ 85643
(520) 824-3560

Grand Canyon
Grand Canyon National Park
P.O. Box 129
Grand Canyon, AZ 86023
(928) 638-7888
www.nps.gov/grca

Organ Pipe Cactus National Monument
Route 1, Box 100
Ajo, AZ 85321
(520) 387-6849 and (520) 387-7661

Saguaro National Monument
3693 South Old Spanish Trail
Tucson, AZ 85730
(520) 733-5158 (Saguaro West)
(520) 733-5153 (Saguaro East)

CALIFORNIA

Death Valley
Death Valley National Monument
Death Valley National Park
P.O. Box 579
Death Valley, CA 92328
(760) 786-3200
www.nps.gov/deva/index.htm

Joshua Tree National Monument
74485 National Park Drive
Twentynine Palms, CA 92277
(760) 367-5500

Mojave National Preserve Desert Information Center
72157 Baker Boulevard
P.O. Box 241
Baker, CA 92309
(760) 733-4040

COLORADO

Dinosaur National Monument
4545 Highway 40
Dinosaur, CO 81610
(970) 374-3000

NEVADA

Great Basin National Park
Baker, NV 89311-9702
(775) 234-7331

NEW MEXICO

Carlsbad Caverns National Park
3225 National Parks Highway
Carlsbad, NM 88220
(505) 785-2232

Bandelier National Monument
HCR 1, Box 1, Suite 15
Los Alamos, NM 87544
(505) 672-0343

Petroglyph National Monument
6001 Unser Boulevard, NW
Albuquerque, NM 87120
(505) 899-0205

White Sands National Monument
P.O. Box 1086
Holloman AFB, NM 88330
(505) 479-6124

TEXAS

Big Bend National Park
P.O. Box 129
Big Bend National Park, TX 79834
(432) 477-2251
www.nps.gov/bibe

Guadalupe Mountains National Park
HC 60 Box 400
Salt Flat, TX 79847
(915) 828-3251

UTAH

Arches National Park
P.O. Box 907
Moab, UT 84532
(435) 719-2299

Bryce Canyon National Park
P.O. Box 170001
Bryce Canyon, UT 84717
(435) 834-5322

Canyonlands National Park
2282 S.W. Resource Boulevard
Moab, UT 84532
(435) 259-7164

Dinosaur National Monument (Quarry)

11625 East 1500 South

Jensen, UT 84035

Zion National Park

SR 9

Springdale, UT 84767

(435) 772-3256

TOURS

Fossil Hunting Trips can be planned through **Jurassic Tours**. They offer guided digs and tours; call (970) 256-0884. Prices range from $65 for half-day trips to $95 for full-day excursions, with discounts for children and groups. The Museum of Western Colorado also schedules digs June through August for $75 per day. Call (888) 488-DINO.

Family Eco-Travel Tours
National Geographic Expeditions hosts many tours under the Family Adventures program. You'll find a wide array of tours in different regions and biomes, including a Family Dinosaur Adventure in Colorado. They also sponsor trips to many national parks in the United States, which include many desert locations. For more information, see www.nationalgeographic.com/ngexpeditions/expeditions_type.html#2.

Calendar of Desert Events

LATE FEBRUARY

Spring wildflowers begin to bloom in Arizona, Nevada, and Texas.

MARCH

Spring wildflowers begin to bloom in California.

Poppies are in full bloom in mid-March in New Mexico.

APRIL

Last chance to catch spring wildflowers in the American deserts.

MAY

Annual Mesa Verde Country Indian Arts & Western Cultural Festival. For more information visit www.swcolo.org/Tourism/iacf.html or call (970) 565-3414.

JUNE

Saguaro bloom in the American deserts.

Take nature walks in the National Parks.

Tehachapi Indian Annual Pow Wow, Tehachapi, California. See Native American dancing, crafts, and food. Call (661) 822-1118 or write to skipper1@lightspeed.net for more information.

JULY

Desert zinnia blooming in Saguaro National Park.

Summer monsoon, or rainy season, begins in the Sonoran Desert.

Celebrate the Naadam Festival, the biggest holiday in Mongolia on July 11. It is celebrated for three days and is known as the Three Manly Games. Historically this was three days of warrior competitions. Today there are wrestling tournaments for men, horse racing for children, and coed archery competitions with blunt arrows. Celebrate with some contests with your friends.

AUGUST

Still time to see the desert zinnias in bloom.

Celebrate Nag Panchami, the Hindu Festival of the Snake.

SEPTEMBER

Summer rainy season ends in the Sonoran Desert.

OCTOBER

Grand Canyon North Rim Visitor Center closes mid-October and reopens mid-May.

Annual Apache Jii Day, in Globe and Miami, Arizona. For more information call (800) 804-5623 or go to www.globemiamichamber.com/events.asp.

Annual Hopi Tuhisma Arts and Crafts Show, Hopi Veteran's Memorial Center, Kykotsmovi, Arizona. Contact Hopi Pu'tuvi at (928) 737-2298 or tuhismamarket@yahoo.com.

DECEMBER

See 6,000 luminaries lit at the Festival of Lights, Sedona, Arizona. Call (928) 282-4838 for more information.

DESERT CHALLENGES

CHAPTER 1

Discovering Deserts

See if you can measure the amount of rainfall that your area gets in a full year, or try measuring the rainfall during just the spring season. Check your local hardware store for a rain gauge. Look in the almanac at your local library for rainfall measurements. How does your area rainfall compare to the rainfall in the Mohave and Sahara deserts?

CHAPTER 2

Welcome to the Wild West

What plant can be as small as a playground ball and as big as a Volkswagon Beetle car? A tumbleweed, of course! Also known as "wind witches" and "Russian thistle," tumbleweeds grow all over American deserts—from Death Valley to the higher mountain elevations. Why do tumbleweeds tumble? It's their way of spreading their seeds. Can you name five other ways that plants spread their seeds?

CHAPTER 3

South of the Border

What happens to seeds that are planted in soil that has a buildup of salt? Find out by planting one seed in normal potting soil and another seed in soil that contains a mixture of two parts potting soil and one part salt. Water both seeds equally. Does the seed in the salty soil grow as well as the seed planted in unsalty soil? Or do you find that the salt dried out the water from the seed and stopped its growth?

CHAPTER 4

Journey to the Sahara, Namib, Kalahari, and Negev

Go to your local zoo and look at the different animals and their habitats. How does each animal's habitat there compare to its natural habitat? How does it differ? What about each animal's diet? Is it just as it is in the wild, or different? How have the animals adapted to their environments?

CHAPTER 5

The Red and Black Deserts of Asia

Visit a library and research the sand of White Sands, New Mexico, in the United States. It is made of another mineral that is almost pure white. Can you find out what mineral makes that sand so white? What is the mineral used for?

CHAPTER 6

Deserts Down Under

The average daily summer temperature in the desert of central Australia is 98° to 102°F (37° to 39°C). How does that compare to some of the other deserts we have visited?

CHAPTER 7

Arabian Days and Nights

Want to share a little taste of Bedouin hospitality? Enjoy a cup of mint tea with a friend. Pour the tea in your own cup first and taste it to show your guest that it is safe. Next, let your friend pour and taste his or her cup. The Bedouin people follow these rules of hospitality when they pour

coffee flavored with cardamom (a licorice-like spice) for their guests, but they also like to drink mint tea.

CHAPTER 8

Not All Deserts Are Hot

Animals have many different ways to keep warm. Blubber keeps animals well insulated from the cold. What other animals have blubber to keep them warm?

CHAPTER 9

Saving the Sands

Chapter 9 has introduced you to many ways to get involved in preserving desert habitats. You can develop some more ways on your own. Get creative. Investigate and learn what else you can do to help preserve deserts and the wildlife that calls these areas home.

Desert Discovery
If you're planning a great conservation project to help preserve desert habitats, contact author Nancy Castaldo at www.nancycastaldo.com. You might see your project listed on her Web site in the future.

INDEX

Rainforests

An Activity Guide for Ages 6–9

Kids go wild for rainforests! These 50-plus games, activities, and experiments are a jungle of fun whether you live near Olympic National Forest in Washington State or the cornfields of Iowa. Young children will delight in exploring the layers of the rainforest, from the forest floor to the canopy, and learning about plants, animals, and people from the temperate rainforests of North America and the tropical rainforests of Southeast Asia, Africa, and South America.

$14.95 (CAN $22.95)

1-55652-476-5

"A potpourri of resources and activity ideas."

—*School Library Journal*

Oceans

An Activity Guide for Ages 6–9

A Smithsonian Notable Book

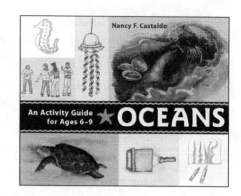

"Using fun activities and games, *Oceans* brilliantly underscores the stewardship that kids have with the oceans."

—Barbara Jeanne Polo, executive director, American Oceans Campaign

"She delights in looking at the ocean from myriad viewpoints and children will enjoy her multifaceted sensibility."

—*School Library Journal*

"Even landlocked students can learn about the ocean and complete the activities in *Oceans*."

—*Curriculum Review*

These more than 50 games, activities, and experiments are a boatful of fun, whether you live in Cape Cod or in Kansas. Young children will delight in exploring different ocean habitats—from tide pools to sunlit waters to the deep-water world where light never penetrates—learning about sharks, sea turtles, dolphins, and much more.

$14.95 (CAN $22.95)

1-55652-443-9

CHICAGO REVIEW PRESS

Distributed by Independent Publishers Group

www.ipgbook.com

Available at your local bookstore or by calling 1-800-888-4741